Cambridge Elements

Elements in Twenty-First Century Music Practice
edited by
Simon Zagorski-Thomas
London College of Music, University of West London

MORE THAN WORDS

Songs for the Language Classroom

Tom Parkinson
University of Kent

Luke Vyner
Creative Listening

Shaftesbury Road, Cambridge CB2 8EA, United Kingdom

One Liberty Plaza, 20th Floor, New York, NY 10006, USA

477 Williamstown Road, Port Melbourne, VIC 3207, Australia

314–321, 3rd Floor, Plot 3, Splendor Forum, Jasola District Centre, New Delhi – 110025, India

103 Penang Road, #05–06/07, Visioncrest Commercial, Singapore 238467

Cambridge University Press is part of Cambridge University Press & Assessment, a department of the University of Cambridge.

We share the University's mission to contribute to society through the pursuit of education, learning and research at the highest international levels of excellence.

www.cambridge.org
Information on this title: www.cambridge.org/9781009662314

DOI: 10.1017/9781009345071

© Tom Parkinson and Luke Vyner 2025

This publication is in copyright. Subject to statutory exception and to the provisions of relevant collective licensing agreements, no reproduction of any part may take place without the written permission of Cambridge University Press & Assessment.

When citing this work, please include a reference to the DOI 10.1017/9781009345071

First published 2025

A catalogue record for this publication is available from the British Library

ISBN 978-1-009-66231-4 Hardback
ISBN 978-1-009-34508-8 Paperback
ISSN 2633-4585 (online)
ISSN 2633-4577 (print)

Additional resources for this publication at www.cambridge.org/Parkinson

Cambridge University Press & Assessment has no responsibility for the persistence or accuracy of URLs for external or third-party internet websites referred to in this publication and does not guarantee that any content on such websites is, or will remain, accurate or appropriate.

More Than Words

Songs for the Language Classroom

Elements in Twenty-First Century Music Practice

DOI: 10.1017/9781009345071
First published online: February 2025

Tom Parkinson
University of Kent

Luke Vyner
Creative Listening

Author for correspondence: Tom Parkinson, t.parkinson@kent.ac.uk

Abstract: English language teachers have long recognised pop songs' potential for engaging students and establishing positive classroom environments that are conducive to language learning. Educational publishers increasingly incorporate music into their coursebooks, including specially commissioned 'ELT songs', whose lyrics feature aspects of the target language. This Element explores the phenomenon of ELT songs from the authors' insider perspective as songwriters. It considers the relationship between music and lyrics in songs, what this means for using songs in the language classroom, the historical developments through which ELT songs emerged, and the contexts in which they are written, listened to, and made. Through literature review and reflection, the authors derive a framework of twelve criteria and ten dilemmas to guide ELT songwriting, before applying it in an analysis of their songs and songwriting process. The final section proposes a model for multidisciplinary collaboration between songwriters and non-musician collaborators including authors, teachers, and publishers.

Keywords: children's music, collaboration, English language teaching, songs, songwriting

© Tom Parkinson and Luke Vyner 2025

ISBNs: 9781009662314 (HB), 9781009345088 (PB), 9781009345071 (OC)
ISSNs: 2633-4585 (online), 2633-4577 (print)

Contents

1 Introduction 1

2 Words and Music 5

3 Contextualising ELT Songs 21

4 Evaluating ELT Songs 38

5 Writing ELT Songs 46

6 Multidisciplinary Collaboration in ELT Songwriting: Specialist, Adaptive, and Relational Expertise 61

References 71

1 Introduction

English is the world's most widely spoken language, the lingua franca of international trade, research, and diplomacy, and the pre-eminent language of globalised popular culture. This status affords significant advantage and opportunity to countries where English is a first language, including in the teaching of English to more than 1.5 billion learners worldwide (Bentley, 2014; Patel, Solly, and Copeland, 2023). Despite growing traction for the notions of 'World Englishes', 'Global English', and 'International English', all of which challenge anglophone countries' assumed authority over the English language (Hamid, 2023; Pennycook, 2017), the multi-billion-dollar English language teaching (ELT) industry still reflects the historical colonial-imperialist hegemony of the UK and the USA and is a major component of Anglosphere countries' soft power (Codó and McDaid, 2019; Knudsen and Markovic, 2021). Each year, British and American publishing houses, including National Geographic, Oxford University Press, and Pearson, produce millions of coursebooks and multimedia resources that are used to teach hundreds of millions of learners across the world. These coursebooks function to standardise the global provision of ELT and retain authority over the English language at the anglophone centre.

Outside of formal education, learners encounter English daily through songs, owing to the ubiquity of anglophone popular music. While many such encounters are passive – hearing songs on television shows or advertisements, for example – they are nonetheless a mainstay of English language learners' life-worlds (Summer, 2018) and can serve as a gateway to active engagement with English language culture, particularly among adolescents. Given the global dominance of anglophone popular music, it is reasonable to assume that English language pop songs account for a large proportion of the estimated 10,000 hours adolescents accrue listening to popular music (Miranda, 2013; Roberts, Henriksen, and Foehr, 2009). Summer (2018), for example, found that German teenagers listened to English language songs for an average of 1.5 hours a day. Like English itself, Anglo-American popular music serves as a vehicle for Western values, products, and, of course, language. Like language education, popular music is a vital component of the UK's, the USA's, and other anglophone countries' export economies and soft power apparatus (Holden, 2013; UK Music, 2021).

This Element sheds light on musical practices that occur at the nexus of ELT and popular music. English language teachers keen to capitalise on their students' passion for popular music have long recognised pop songs' potential to support learning and have explored songs' pedagogical affordances in their classrooms. Educational publishers, too, increasingly incorporate music into their syllabi, including what are known as 'ELT songs' – songs composed *specifically for* ELT contexts. Typically, ELT songs are written in Western pop vernaculars with lyrics that feature aspects of the target language including grammar, lexis, idioms, and pronunciation. Educational resources first and foremost, ELT songs arguably lack the authenticity of songs encountered by learners in naturalistic settings. However, they avoid the potentially hazardous features associated with 'real' pop songs, such as erroneous grammar, slang vernaculars, and adult themes, which can discourage teachers from incorporating songs into their classroom teaching.

We, the authors, have professional backgrounds in the music and education sectors, having worked at different points in our careers as songwriters, composers, and teachers. These normally discrete career pathways converged in 2015 when we secured a contract to write ELT songs for a major British publisher, and we have since developed a portfolio of more than 200 published ELT songs. While our musical and educational backgrounds equipped us with the basic skills and understanding necessary to undertake this work, we soon realised that the creative practices, professional values, and expectations associated with songwriting and language education do not always align straightforwardly. Musical decision-making based on intuition and aesthetic judgement can be thwarted by the rigidity of linguistic requirements, and playful strategies for idea generation can jar with the more disciplined working norms of non-musical collaborators. Over time, however, the linguistic, musical, and pedagogical imperatives guiding the work became points of negotiation, balance, and compromise, in discussion with collaborators and stakeholders. Through these negotiations, we developed our music practice of ELT songwriting, replete with its own compositional strategies, formal conventions, and normative aesthetics.

The practice of ELT songwriting sits within a wider field of mutually contingent music practices, comprising musical language teaching (teachers using songs in their classrooms), musical language learning (students learning language by listening to and/or performing music), and musical curriculum design (the commissioning and programming of songs for educational purposes). These practices are engaged in by millions globally, yet they occur in spaces that would not ordinarily be considered musical spaces. Most participants in this field are not trained musicians, and musical aims are seen as incidental to non-musical ones.

Despite music's secondary status in an ELT context, choosing to use songs to teach English is fundamentally a *musical* decision because it is predicated on songs' added musical value over other texts. However, research into language teacher cognition suggests that teachers' use of songs is rarely underpinned by an informed understanding of *how* songs function to support language acquisition; rather, it stems from an intuitive or experience-based conviction that they do (see Section 3.4). Still less is known about the reasoning behind ELT songs' characteristics – their form, genre, tempo, timbre, arrangement, mix, and other factors – and how these relate to pedagogical aims and learner experiences. To address this knowledge gap, in this Element we generate insight into the common but little-understood phenomenon of ELT songs, through an emic investigation of ELT songwriting and production.

1.1 Contribution to Knowledge

This Element sits across the domains of songwriting and ELT, and we anticipate that it will interest practitioners and scholars of both. Moreover, its original contributions to knowledge are of potential value to scholars working in cognate areas, including but not limited to the study of creative practice, practice-led research, applied linguistics, interdisciplinary collaboration, and the creative industries.

To our knowledge, this Element is the first in-depth study of the ELT song phenomenon. Despite there being an established literature surrounding the use of songs in language teaching, almost all studies concern the use of commercial pop songs in the classroom as opposed to songs composed *for* the classroom (for exceptions, see Lee and Schreibeis, 2021; Legg, 2009; Ludke, 2018). For the field of ELT, then, this Element addresses a conspicuous absence in the literature, helping to bring research into line with practice. Another gap that we address is the dearth of attention afforded to the role of music (as opposed to lyrics) in song-based learning and teaching. Most existing studies of song use in ELT build their theoretical frameworks through engagement with pedagogical and applied linguistics literatures and/or insights from ELT practice, and seldom engage with work in the fields of popular music studies, musicology, or the psychology of music. We seek to establish points of intersection across these literatures. Finally, in documenting and reflecting on our ELT songwriting practice, we generate fresh insight into the phenomenon of the ELT song from an insider perspective, enabling a richer understanding of the perceptions, values, and beliefs underpinning the ELT song field.

For music and related disciplines, this Element broadens the contextual and theoretical scope of songwriting scholarship through its focus on an established but lesser-known domain of songwriting whose underpinning priorities, constraints, and norms differ from those which dominate the existing songwriting literature. We present ELT songwriting as a practice of writing to brief, where both process and product are contingent on extra-musical decision-making and where musical values are ancillary to strict linguistic and pedagogical criteria. Furthermore, ELT songs are composed for children, and ELT songwriting is therefore governed by a matrix of thematic, moral, aesthetic, and temporal constraints and imperatives associated with childhood and adolescence. Moreover, beyond its specific context, ELT songwriting serves as a case study for less glamorous songwriting *work* (Long and Barber, 2015) that often constitutes a major, main, or even sole income stream for professional songwriters, but is under-represented in songwriting research.

1.2 Methodology and Approach

Our approach to researching and writing this Element is best described as practice-*led*, as opposed to practice-*based* or practice-*as*-research (Nelson, 2006). Like any creative endeavour, our songwriting practice involves finding solutions to problems, but it does not follow a predetermined research agenda wherein the practice itself constitutes an inductive research method. Furthermore, while our practice generates creative outputs – ELT songs – these are not research outputs through which new knowledge is shared with scholarly and practitioner audiences. Rather, they are commercial, task-oriented products for a defined purpose and user community.

However, the impetus to write better ELT songs and the desire to understand what constitutes a good ELT song are both practice-*led*, and the questions, problems, and challenges encountered over several years of songwriting practice are the basis for the lines of enquiry pursued across the different sections of this Element. What exactly *are* songs? How do music and lyrics relate to one another in the context of a song and what are the implications of this relationship for language teaching? How do ELT songs differ from other types of song? How are they experienced in the classroom and where do they sit in the wider context of the ELT industry? What do teachers, learners, and other stakeholders need and expect from ELT songs? And, most importantly, how can we write ELT songs that are effective, enjoyable, and fit for purpose?

We have attempted to answer these questions in three ways: deductively, by reviewing existing research and practice; abductively, through reflecting on our ongoing practice; and inductively, by eliciting the compositional stories inherent in artefacts (our songs) (Mäkelä, 2007). Undertaking this project alongside our ongoing songwriting practice provided a basis for embedded critical reflection throughout, supporting evidence-based practice and practice-led research.

1.3 Outline

Sections 2 and 3 offer an in-depth investigation into what ELT songs *are*. In Section 2, we unpack the nature of songs as linguistic and musical texts, as an oral–aural phenomenon, and as recorded sound, and explore the relationships among songs' lyrical, musical, and sonic aspects and the implications of these relationships for the use of songs in language teaching. In Section 3, we focus on ELT songs as a specific genre of song, outlining the historical developments out of which they have emerged and situating them in relation to the current contexts in which they are written, listened to, and made.

Sections 4, 5, and 6 centre on the practice of ELT songwriting. In Section 4, we consider the perspectives and expectations of different stakeholders involved in the commissioning, production, use, and reception of ELT songs and propose a set of evaluative criteria for 'good' ELT songs that balance different stakeholders' priorities. We also identify some compositional dilemmas that arise when attempting to reconcile linguistic, pedagogical, and musical aims and priorities. In Section 5, we explore these dilemmas through examples from our own practice and reflect critically on our work and creative process in light of insights from earlier sections. In the final, short section, Section 6, we propose a model for ELT songwriting as a relational and multidisciplinary process distinct from other forms of songwriting and identify areas for further research.

2 Words and Music

As explained in Section 1, ELT songs are songs written for use in another musical practice – the teaching of English through music. Notwithstanding this specific purpose, however, they are also *just songs*. Because songs are a primordial phenomenon of human culture, and a ubiquitous feature of our everyday lives, it is rare outside of musicology for their generic nature to be interrogated phenomenologically. In other words, ordinary listeners enjoy songs, and may well discuss and even analyse individual songs, but they do not usually concern themselves with the question of what songs *are*, because they know intuitively.[1] This includes ELT teachers, curriculum designers, and young learners, most of whom are musically untrained. As a result, there is little understanding of, or attention given to, what actually occurs cognitively, emotionally, physiologically, and socioculturally when learners listen to a song. Yet research suggests that these dimensions are central to songs' efficacy in engaging learners and supporting their language acquisition and skills development, and also to teachers' rationales for using songs in the classroom (which we discuss in Sections 3 and 4). We therefore begin this section by considering the nature of songs – their properties, their reception, and their role in human life – and what this might mean for the use, and in our case composition, of songs for language teaching.

---

[1] Though what constitutes 'song' differs across global cultures and traditions.

2.1 What Are Songs?

Songs are musical compositions that combine words and music, and are usually sung; that is, songs are usually projected into the world by the human voice, which shapes their melodic, rhythmic, dynamic, timbral, and phonological contours and thus imbues them with musical and linguistic meaning. Like all vocal utterances, a song manifests as sound through disturbances in air pressure from the point of leaving the singer's mouth, creating acoustic waves that are later received by the listener's ear. The listener's auricle amplifies the acoustic waves and funnels them down the ear canal, where they strike the listener's ear drum. Thereafter they reverberate through the ossicle bones and into the listener's fluid-filled cochlea, whose thousands of hair cells send neurochemical signals to the brain via the auditory nerve. The auditory cortex processes these signals, recognising pitch and dynamics, and parsing out language and music. Through perceptive and cognitive mechanisms distributed across several regions of the brain, this new musical and linguistic input interfaces with the listener's prior knowledge, generating emotional and cognitive meaning.

Songs are therefore profoundly physiological (Chesebro et al., 1985) and intimately associated with their singers' voices. The voice connotes selfhood, identity, and expression, particularly of emotions (Cavarero, 2005). Composers and performers of songs exploit the expressive potential of the voice to achieve levels of emotional intensity unattainable through speech, which has more restricted tonal and dynamic ranges.[2]

As a point of departure, then, four key issues have arisen that have implications for the use, creation, and reception of ELT songs. Firstly, while songs are used in the language classroom to teach language, they are multimodal texts with linguistic and musical aspects. Secondly, songs' principal manifestation is *as sound*. Thirdly, songs are vehicles for the expression of identity and emotion, particularly through the singer's voice. Fourthly, although speech and song both issue from the human voice, speaking and singing are not the same. Let us now consider each of these issues in turn.

2.2 Songs as Musical and Linguistic Texts

As compositions comprising words and music, songs are both literary and musical (Bennett, 2012). These are not discrete, parallel aspects; rather, songs' meanings derive from the complex interaction between linguistic and musical systems, and the different levels within each system (Bickford, 2007). As such, while a language teacher deploying a song in the classroom might

---

[2] With the possible exception of tonal languages.

understandably think only of its literary dimension, students listening to the song are prone to the semantically generative interaction between music and language and derive unique perceptual, cognitive, and emotional experiences from it.

Privileging songs' lyrical aspect in an ELT context is of course rational and intuitive. However, while the music of a song is certainly ancillary to lyrics in an ELT context, there are hazards to overlooking the importance of music to learners' experiences, and significant affordances to incorporating music more substantially in language pedagogy. An informed awareness of how language and music interact in songs and are processed by the brain to derive meaning can support teachers, curriculum designers, and in our case ELT songwriters to foster more engaging, inclusive, and effective learning environments.

Before considering their interaction in the context of song, though, let us first consider some inherent commonalities between language and music. Both are systems of communication used to convey information between humans. Sounds function in both language and music as communicative signals (Kumar et al., 2022). Both make use of variations in duration, pitch, and (in the case of speech and vocal music) the shape of the oral cavity to distinguish among signals within their systems. Both entail the ordering of learnt signals into hierarchical structures to communicate more sophisticated meanings. As alluded to earlier, both language and music share physiological, neurological, and cognitive resources in their production, reception, and processing (Patel, 2012). Fast-moving empirical work exploring the commonalities between music and language, particularly in cognitive neuroscience, follows centuries of speculative rumination on music's resembling a form of language. While, as Patel (2008) observes, analogies equating music to language can be superficial, this long speculative tradition highlights that we *intuit* a profound commonality between the two, even if our understanding of that commonality is limited. Finally, both are common to all human cultures (Nettl, 2000), and humans' ability to make musical and linguistic sense of sound sets us apart from all other species (Patel, 2008).

However, there are important differences between language and music, particularly in relation to meaning production, that are highly relevant to the use of songs in the language classroom. These become most apparent when we consider the relationship between form and function. Zbikowski (2012) noted consensus among cognitive linguists that grammar – the linguistic organising system that supports communication – works through *constructions*, described by Goldberg (2003) as 'stored pairings of form and function, including morphemes, words [and] idioms' (p. 219, quoted in Zbikowski, 2012, p. 126). The form of these constructions both determines and enacts their functions.

Crucially, the relationship between form and function in language is learnable and thus establishes a 'shared referential frame' that supports language's primary function of directing others' attention to objects or events, 'mak[ing] possible cooperative behaviour' and 'setting out a framework of shared intentionality' (Zbikowski, 2012, pp. 128–129). On this basis, an individual can communicate, say, a recipe for lasagne by encoding its ingredients, processes, and environmental requirements in linguistic constructions that will be readily understood by others provided they share the same referential frame (i.e., the same language). This also allows for translation between *different* languages. English and Arabic, for example, both have signifiers for objects and processes (e.g., *tomato*, طماطم) and organising grammars that can be learnt and interfaced, allowing for our lasagne recipe to be communicated from one language to another within a shared, interlingual referential frame.

Like language, music is composed of formal constructions that become characteristic of genres and repertoires and can be recognised, taught, and replicated. However, unlike in language, the communicative functions paired to musical forms are not clear. Even if a performer and a listener share a referential frame (an understanding of rondo form or the Phrygian mode, for example), musical constructions cannot communicate intentionality to the same degree. Put simply, one cannot communicate a lasagne recipe with music.

Furthermore, music cannot be 'translated' to provide differently enculturated listeners with a precisely equivalent experience.[3] While some features of music are thought to be common across musical cultures, others are culturally specific, and universal or common 'meanings' cannot be transmitted across music cultures like they can in language (Becker, 1986). Rather, as Patel (2008) argued, when a piece of music is 'translated' into the tonal or rhythmic structures or instrument families of another musical culture, its meanings are fundamentally altered.

In its ability to communicate intended, specific meanings within and across culture groups, language is therefore 'functionally unique among the phenomena of culture' (Bickford, 2007, p. 440). Yet music's perennial and universal presence in human life attests to its having meaning, and its usage in social settings, whether deliberate or incidental, demonstrates its important communicative function. What, then, does music *mean* and what meanings does it communicate?

Patel (2008) argued that one aspect of musical meaning is purely formal. Where linguistic meaning is inextricable from its arbitrary referential frame, music can be meaningful to listeners purely because the structural logic of

---

[3] Dell and Elmedlaoui (2008, cited in Turbin and Strebbins, 2010) use the term 'enculturated listener' analogously to the notion of 'native speaker' to refer to insiders of musical cultures.

a given unit (e.g., piece, phrase, passage) engenders musical expectation relating to 'auditory universals', 'style-specific aspects', and 'piece-specific regularities' (Patel, 2008, p. 305). The fulfilment, denial, and delay of expectations combine to generate emotional responses in listeners.

We return to the significance of emotion for song use in language teaching in Section 2.4. For now, let us consider further the structural logics of music and language via the concept of coherence relations (Wolf and Gibson, 2005). In linguistics, coherence relations refer to the extent to which segments within a linguistic whole fit together in a way that makes sense to a listener or reader. The impression of coherence depends on each segment playing a role in communicating an intended meaning. Linguistic meaning unfolds over time through the linear ordering of segments, establishing what we know as narrative.

The logic of music, too, depends on coherence relations between segments, though, as we have already established, the impression of coherence in music corresponds not to 'arbitrary, specific semantic reference(s)' (Patel, 2008, p. 328) but to formal expectations. From Wolf and Gibson's (2005) framework of eight relations among clauses, Patel (2008) identified six as being common to music: *similarity*, *contrast*, *elaboration*, *cause–effect*, *violated expectation*, and *temporal sequence* (p. 338). For example, musical pieces feature recurring melodic phrases or chord progressions (*similarity*), and subsequent phases and progressions that provide *contrast*; sequences of segments can establish a sense of *cause and effect* (the anticipation of melodic descent after a sustained period of ascent, for example); and so on. Patel's (2008) analysis thus highlights that despite there being significant differences in linguistic and musical meaning, there are also similarities in how segments relate to one another in language and music, and in how these relations establish a sense of coherent narrative.

However, despite these acknowledged similarities, there are surprisingly few studies exploring coherence relations in the context of songs. Songs rely on linguistic and musical narratives, and the overlaying of linguistic and musical structural systems places them in interaction and creates mutual contingencies and affordances. Consider, for example, two linguistic segments whose coherence relationship is one of *similarity*, such as 'I like chicken' / 'I like pizza'. Now, imagine a song in which these linguistic segments are set against musical segments whose relationship is one of stark contrast or violated expectation – an eccentric modulation or time signature change, for example. The combined narrative of the song would be very different from that of the lyrics or music in isolation because the music would imbue the 'pizza' with a sense of dissonance, undermining the consonance of the lyric and establishing a sense of ambiguity. On the other hand, if lyrics feature starkly contrasting segments (such as 'I used to love her' / 'now I hate her'), their narrative coherence can be reinforced by musical segments that also contrast starkly. Among the songwriter's tasks, then, is to establish something akin to coherence relations *across* lyrics and music, in order to synergise the meaning-making properties of both. While some songwriters might use the juxtaposition of lyrics against 'contrasting' musical properties as a more advanced compositional device (e.g., to imply irony, humour, etc.), ELT songwriters in particular should avoid ambiguity or dissonance between lyrics and music in order to create readily apprehensible songs.

Furthermore, because coherence relations in music are based on expectation (whether style-specific, piece-specific, or auditory universal – see Patel, 2008), the overlaying of lyrics onto musical structures can give rise to expectations concerning the relationship between lyrical segments, and indeed to segments' structural properties. This interdependence of musical and linguistic structures has clear implications for the language classroom, in terms of both how listener-learners process songs and how songs can be employed pedagogically. Let us explore this via the example of twelve-bar blues.

Twelve-bar blues derived from African American song forms and is foundational to many jazz and popular music genres. As its name suggests, it comprises twelve *bars* – units of musical time comprising a specified number of beats – arranged into three sections of four bars, each associated with a lyrical line. Harmonically, twelve-bar blues is typically arranged predominantly across tonic (I), subdominant (IV), and dominant (V) chords.

Owing to both the pervasive influence of American popular culture and twelve-bar blues' structural simplicity and regularity, it has become a globally recognised form. We might therefore reasonably assume some degree of familiarity among young language learners in many international contexts, at least sufficient to generate style-specific expectations in terms of form and harmonic structure. The lyrics of twelve-bar blues also tend to follow a standardised structure, in which the first line is sung over the first four-bar section, usually[4] set to the tonic (I) chord (though the line often starts with an *anacrusis* in the last bar of the preceding section), with the final syllable typically beginning on the first beat of the third bar. The same line is then repeated over the next four-bar section, usually comprising two bars set to the subdominant (IV) chord and two bars set back to the tonic (I). The third and final line is usually an elaboration of the earlier, repeated line, and ends the verse. Subsequent verses will often build on the first, following the same lyrical structure. Harmonically it usually comprises two bars of the dominant (V) and two bars of the tonic (I), though it is common for the final bar to be split across the tonic (I) and the dominant (V) (known as the 'turnaround').

---

[4] It is also common for the second bar to move to the subdominant (IV).

In the bringing together of words and music in a twelve-bar blues piece, we see not only the overlaying of musical and linguistic structures but also the interaction of the processes of meaning-making associated with music and language, as discussed earlier. The learnt, style-specific formal norms (the twelve-bar structure and its inherent tonal tensions and resolutions) and piece-specific regularities (the repetition of the rhythmic and melodic phrasing of the vocal line) generate expectation of what is to come as the piece progresses. Concomitantly, the lyrics are distributed across repeated or similar (lines one and two) and elaborative (line three) units. In this way, the linguistic and musical coherence relations in twelve-bar blues songs are mutually contingent. What is most salient in the context of language pedagogy is that the structural expectations issuing from musical form also generate *linguistic* expectation. That is, a learner-listener familiar with twelve-bar blues will likely anticipate *similarity* (i.e., a repeated line) at the beginning of bar five and *elaboration* at bar nine and will also prepare themselves for a further round of similarity and elaboration at the end of the twelve bars (particularly if the song features the 'turnaround'). They will also develop expectations regarding the length and metre of linguistic units. As such, twelve-bar blues has pedagogical value for prompting anticipation through the coherence relations inherent to its musical form, and by providing a regular framework with inherent repetition and familiar spacings that serve as rhythmically stable lead-ins to units of language.

Twelve-bar blues is just one of many common structural formulae. Popular music is highly formulaic in terms of the ordering of sections (e.g., verse, chorus, bridge), section lengths (e.g., eight- or sixteen-bar verses), chord sequencing (e.g., I, V, vi, IV), and lyric placement (e.g., four lines per verse, two bars per line, choruses repeated). As with twelve-bar blues, we can therefore assume a high degree of intuitive familiarity among learners, which will lead to expectations in terms of how songs unfold musically and, consequently, lyrically, owing to the overlaying of musical and lyrical coherence relations. Songs' narrative logic, inherent repetitions, and stability in terms of tempo, rhythm, and metre offer an intuitive and pedagogically versatile framework that can be exploited for teaching language. Adherence to familiar and intuitive formulae is a key concern in our work as ELT songwriters, though this has to be balanced with factors such as novelty and surprise (unmet expectations) which can be central to a song's appeal.

2.3 Songs as Recorded Sound

So far, we have considered songs' status as sound only in relation to singing. Understandably, vocal features are usually the sole aural focus in literature concerning songs in language teaching contexts. Rarely are non-vocal dimensions of music accounted for, beyond passing consideration of genre choice or recommendations for music to be 'of reasonable musical and aesthetic quality' (Summer, 2018, pp. 203–204). However, songs used in ELT are usually polyphonic compositions, featuring instrumental and vocal parts, and are usually phonographic (recorded) and reproduced acousmatically (through speakers) as amplified sound. These features have auditory, semantic, affective, and pedagogical implications that should be accounted for when using, choosing, or composing songs for the language classroom.

In Section 2.1, we discussed the physiological processes involved in the production and reception of vocal sound, and the unmediated, embodied connection established between performer and listener through material disturbances in air pressure. In an acousmatic context, however, a performer's voice is mediated by recording and amplification technologies that can radically alter the qualities of a sound source. At a straightforward auditory level, a poor recording can negatively impact the clarity and intelligibility of singing or speech by altering or obscuring the consonant and vowel sounds from which syllables are composed. The significance of this for language teaching is obvious.

However, the deliberate manipulation of recorded sound is integral to the practice of record production, a domain in which the aim of accurately 'capturing' auditory scenes has long been usurped by that of simulating or inventing sonic events and environments. Within an invented environment, a record producer has control over which sounds and sonic qualities are prioritised and foregrounded. Using specialist technologies, they can also easily circumvent the intrinsic and environmental factors that constrain and hierarchise acoustic sounds, such as a singer's maximum volume or the presence of background noise.

One result of this process is the illusion of spatial distance. If a producer records an adult and a child singing, then mixes the child lower (quieter) than the adult and attenuates the higher frequencies of the child's voice using equalisation (EQ), the child will sound farther away. The illusion of space can be further achieved through the application of effects such as reverb and delay, which simulate the reflection and decay of sound in physical spaces, and also by distributing sounds across the stereo field to simulate the directionality of sounds in a physical environment (i.e., the location of a sound source in relation to the listener). This can have a significant impact on auditory scene analysis – the process by which our auditory system segregates sound sources into streams that can be processed in isolation. Furthermore, within this creative paradigm, sonic properties that are prized in communicative settings, such as clarity and audibility, can also be *deliberately eschewed* for aesthetic reasons (or, alternatively, negated owing to poor craftsmanship). This, too, can impact auditory scene analysis.

As a consequence of these and other sonic manipulations, recorded songs feature auditory scenes that differ markedly from those encountered in 'real' physical environments, and crucially are intended for different listening practices from those of communicative settings or, indeed, listening for comprehension in the language classroom. This should be acknowledged and accommodated when choosing songs for use in the language classroom and when designing corresponding learning activities. However, this might not always be a case of selecting songs with the most natural-sounding environments; if learners are to develop the skills required to listen to and interpret songs *as an authentic genre of text* they encounter daily (Summer, 2018), then there is a case for incorporating *unnatural* sonic environments that reflect the norms of popular music at large. The competing priorities of realism and aesthetic normativity present a dilemma for songwriters and producers of songs for the language classroom.

Beyond audition, recording and amplification processes can alter a performer's voice semantically. Where no acoustic sound source is present, listeners instead imagine the performer – that is, they construct their identity based on cues encoded in the sound of their voice, which can correspond to assumptions about gender, race, nationality, regionality, class, age, and location. In altering the dynamic, timbral, tonal, and spatial qualities of a voice, the recording and amplification processes therefore have the potential to alter the cues that inform the listener's construction of the performer's identity.

Furthermore, the ability to mix naturally quieter sounds above louder ones allows for acoustically quieter styles of singing that are dynamically (and therefore aesthetically) closer to speech than open-voiced singing styles developed for large acoustic environments. Some of the expressive features of these quieter styles, such as faltering, gasping, and whispering, can resemble suprasegmentals – features of speech that betray emotional states, determine utterance type (e.g., question, exclamation), and communicate features of intended meaning such as sarcasm, secrecy, or doubt (see Section 2.5). For example, in the opening verse of the Beatles' 'You've Got to Hide Your Love Away' (1965), John Lennon's almost whispered, croaking vocal is mixed so as to be audible above a backing track of vigorously strummed acoustic guitars, bass guitar, maracas, and tambourine. This foregrounds cues relating to energy level and emotional state which a listener may factor into their construction of the singer-protagonist's identity (Askerøi, 2013; Zagorski-Thomas, 2014).

In summary, then, the recording process (and the performance styles made possible by recording) can impart layers of meaning onto the human voice that interact with the literary meanings of songs' lyrics. While this might potentially present problems in a language classroom context, it also offers affordances in terms of 'music-mediated language experiences' (Cores-Bilbao et al., 2019, p. 2). For example, a teacher might encourage learners to pay attention to the emotional or identity cues in a singer's voice, thereby making explicit and collective the otherwise tacit and individual process of identity construction, and to factor these into their collective interpretations of songs' meanings. Such activities have been proposed as a means to initiate the co-construction of meaning in the classroom, to foster group cohesion and develop learners' socio-emotional awareness and interpersonal competencies (Cores-Bilbao et al., 2019).

As Askerøi (2013) notes, identity categories are signalled not through the voice alone 'but [also] through the ways in which the effect of that voice is impacted by sonic markers in the musical backdrop' (p. 16). Tropes deriving from instrumental arrangement, or the sonic environment invented through production, become associated with certain communities, thereby 'acquir[ing] an ideological meaning about belonging to or rebelling against these communities' (Zagorski-Thomas, 2014, p. 140) which can have a significant bearing on how they are received by listeners – including, in our case, young learners.

As we discuss in more detail in Section 3, young people's musical preferences are intimately tied to the construction of individual and group identities (Baker, 2001; Bonneville-Roussy et al., 2013; Herbert and Dibben, 2018; Lamont and Hargreaves, 2019), and young adolescents in particular experience a narrowing of preferences and strong feelings of dislike for music outside of those preferences. It is possible therefore that a song's sonic environment might provoke strong feelings of dislike among learners owing to social associations, or might appeal to some learners and not/more than others and thereby undermine the positive learning environments and social cohesion that songs can engender (which we discuss in Section 2.4). On the other hand, attention to learners' preferences can support the selection of songs that engage learners and enhance those aspects. As ELT songwriters, we have to pay careful attention to our songs' production, in terms of how we render individual voices (from both purely auditory and semantic perspectives), how we simulate space, and how we achieve an engaging and inclusive aesthetic that corresponds to the preferences of learners themselves.

Askerøi (2013) highlighted that meanings can be imparted in a popular song through what he called 'sonic markers', 'expressive devices in music that range from vocal peculiarities to instrumental stylings and the technological aspects of production' (p. 2). These devices are *marked* by their association with time, place, or space within the history of recorded popular music. Because of their historical contextual situatedness, sonic markers can signify the past, present, and future, and evoke real, mythical, remembered, and imagined places. For example, a song might signify 1990s Seattle through markers of guitar timbre or tone (overdriven, muddy), harmonic idiom (a sequence of four power chords), and so on.

Importantly, Askerøi (2013) emphasised that sonic markers do not signify in isolation. Rather, a song's musical backdrop 'attenuates the message contained in the lyrics and vocal performance' (Askerøi, 2013, p. 31) and must therefore be interpreted in relation to the song's other elements. By corollary, since lyrics are attenuated by their musical backdrop, analysis of a song's meaning should not rely on lyrics alone and should attend to the narrative function of the sonic markers. Again, this presents further affordances for music-mediated language experiences (Cores-Bilbao et al., 2019); incorporating activities that direct learners' attention to sonic features has the potential to enrich their interpretation of songs and develop their socio-emotional awareness and interpersonal competencies. As songwriters and producers, we intuitively seek to align sonic markers with lyrics. When working in an ELT context, however, this occurs at a more deliberate level, often in collaboration with, or in response to feedback from, curriculum authors. We discuss our use of sonic markers in Section 5.

It is interesting to consider the extent to which the signification of sonic markers depends on lived experience or learnt awareness of their historicity – to what extent, for example, does a 'surf guitar' sound evoke nostalgia for 1960s Southern California among listeners born in 1990s London? – and therefore whether they would resonate with children in global language classrooms. Research suggests that lived experience is not necessary for the development of musical memory. Van Dijck (2006) asserted that 'recorded music is vital to the construction of personal *and collective* cultural memory' (p. 358, our emphasis) and that these memory types are mutually constituted; by sharing and talking about our personal preferences and experiences, we develop 'collective reservoirs of recorded music that "stick to the mind" and . . . become our cultural heritage' (p. 369). Meanwhile, collectively constructed meanings are 'transposed onto individual memory, resulting in an intricate mixture of recall and imagination [even where] remembrance cannot be rooted in actual lived experience' (Van Dijck, 2006, p. 363). This again highlights both the extent to which musical meaning is socially constructed and the role of music in fostering community and social cohesion. By incorporating recorded music into children's education and life-worlds, including in classroom settings, adults are engaging children in processes of memory formation and inculcating them into a collective cultural reservoir.

Two final salient features of recorded music are its fixity (Maloy, 2018) and its resulting replicability/repeatability. Unlike live music, whose every rendition is unique, recorded music is always already an historical artefact and the same recorded performance is reproduced each time it is sounded. This is relevant for two reasons. Firstly, a recording's repeatability has obvious utility in a classroom context because repetition supports memorisation, and activities involving songs invariably incorporate repetition. Secondly, and related to our earlier discussion of sonic marking, the fixity of a recorded song means that it can never change. Therefore, ELT songs cannot be modified or refined once they have been recorded and may become redundant or dated. In the ELT songwriting process, the fixed nature of songs prompts concerns about currency and longevity, and how songs might be 'future-proofed' for the intended lifespan of a syllabus or resource.

2.4 Songs and Emotion

As noted in Section 2.2, a key dimension of musical meaning relates to music's ability to communicate emotions. The emotional impact of music is also among the most prominent of the supported justifications for using songs in the language classroom. Researchers and practitioners have long valued songs' ability to evoke positive emotions and thereby reduce anxiety (Dolean, 2016; Dolean and Dolean, 2014), increase motivation (Ajibade and Ndububa, 2008; Chou, 2014; Fernández de Cañete García, Pineda, and Waddell, 2022; Kumar et al., 2022; Kuśnierek, 2016; Murphey, 2013; Tegge, 2018), and improve second language (L2) learning/acquisition (Chen and Chen, 2009; Chou, 2014). However, few studies pay close attention to the *nature* of songs' emotional impact. Closer examination of the ways in which music stimulates emotions offers important transferable insights into how young language learners respond to songs, with implications for how the decisions concerning the characteristics of songs (whether in composition or in selection), and the ways in which they are used pedagogically, impact the learning environment and learners' experiences.

Patel (2008) observes that, unlike language, music can generate emotional meaning through form alone. Experimental studies have, albeit to varying degrees, identified consistent associations between defined musical structures and particular physiological responses associated with emotion, such as chills, tears, and lumps in the throat (see Kaminska and Woolf, 2000, for a review). Kaminska and Woolf (2000) argued that these relationships provide 'clear evidence that musical attributes can inform emotional reaction' (p. 133). However, such emotional responses have been differentiated from 'everyday' emotions such as jealousy, relief, excitement, or boredom, on the basis that, while they can be intense, they are unvalenced – that is, they have neither positive nor negative connotation (Hunter and Schellenberg, 2010). Others have differentiated between 'true' emotions based on subjective appraisal of events, and the 'moods' or 'aesthetic emotions' evoked by music (see Juslin, 2013).

Juslin and Västfjäll (2008), however, posited that music can indeed induce valenced emotions through mechanisms other than appraisal. They proposed six further mechanisms by which music induces emotion: *evaluative conditioning*, whereby a piece of music induces emotion because it has been repeatedly paired with an emotionally valenced stimulus such as a happy event, even if the listener is not consciously aware of the connection; *brain stem reflex* and *musical expectation*, both of which are associated with intrinsic musical features; *emotional contagion*, whereby listeners perceive an emotional expression in the music and then subconsciously mimic that expression to the point of inducing (i.e., feeling) the emotion; *visual imagery*, whereby mental imagery stimulated by the music triggers emotions in the listener; and *episodic memory*, whereby music evokes a memory which induces the emotions associated with it.

While Juslin and Västfjäll's (2008) focus is instrumental music, their framework is nonetheless relevant to the use of songs. Firstly, it highlights that music not only communicates but actually induces emotion in listeners. Children and adolescents display high levels of emotionality (Guyer, Silk, and Nelson, 2016) and are thus highly susceptible – vulnerable even – to the emotional impact of music. Those with influence over children's musical encounters must therefore account for music's emotional potency as part of their duty of care.

Secondly, according to Juslin and Västfjäll's (2008) framework, learners' emotional responses to music depend heavily on conscious and subconscious association. Care should therefore also be taken in the pairing of music with non-musical stimuli. This includes lyrics, but may also include other texts, images, videos, or events, all of which can contribute valence to the often-intense emotional arousal induced by music. Furthermore, music used in classrooms may invoke children's memories of past experiences, or even intergenerational memories (including trauma), leading to unanticipated emotional responses.

Finally, the group-cohesive function of music identified by Juslin and Västfjäll (2008) is particularly relevant to the language classroom, a vibrant social setting in which human beings grow and develop together, interacting collectively with their environment and with one another. As noted at the outset of this section, researchers and practitioners have long valued songs' ability to evoke positive emotions and thereby enhance learning environments. In a song, language provides a communicative framework for directing attention and sharing intentions, while music supports the sharing of feelings within groups and, at a culture group level, *between* groups (Patel, 2008). This is pertinent both to the increasingly culturally diverse school populations of many international contexts and to the growing emphasis on promoting intercultural awareness in education globally. On this basis alone, a strong deductive case can be made not only for using songs in the language classroom but also for taking their musical aspect seriously. If songs induce emotional responses in learners, and positive emotions engender engaged learning environments that are conducive to language learning, and our principal aim is to promote language learning, then we should take care to select (or, in our case, compose) songs that induce positive emotional responses through the considered pairing of music, lyrics, and other extra-musical and non-linguistic stimuli. In Section 2.5, we turn our attention to another aspect of the nature of song that is highly relevant, but under-interrogated, in the context of language teaching – the relationship between singing and speech.

2.5 Singing versus Speech

A singer enacts the melodic, rhythmic, and dynamic contours of a song's vocal line through the same neural, skeletal, and muscular functions that a speaker uses to shape phonemes into spoken words (speech). Moreover, because vocal lines are almost always verbal, the singer simultaneously imbues the sound of their voice with musical and phonological form to communicate both musical and linguistic meaning. Vowels, the nucleus of linguistic syllables formed by opening the vocal tract, are the main pitch-bearing units in songs (Turpin and Stebbins, 2010), while consonants, which begin and/or end syllables by obstructing or constraining airflow, act as injunctions to mark metre and rhythm.

While speech is primarily a means of communicating language through sound, the spoken voice also conveys emotional meaning through its textural, dynamic, and tonal qualities, much like music. Speech and song thus share many fundamental similarities, but, like music and language, they are not the same. In this section, we consider the relationship between singing and speech, and the implications of this relationship for the creation of songs for ELT contexts. While there is some inevitable overlap with the discussion of the relationship between music and language in Section 2.1, our focus here is primarily on sound and syntax, rather than semantics or cognition.

Turpin and Stebbins (2010) observed that because songs feature the voice as a musical instrument, and because the voice also produces spoken language, we are prone to seeing song as derivative of speech. The lyrical convention common to many song traditions of a first-person singular protagonist ('I') addressing a second-person singular interlocutor ('you'), which depicts an intimate one-to-one exchange, also contributes to an understanding of song as a form of speech. These features belie the fact that songs are in fact a heavily stylised genre of one-to-many communication that, although oral, are also *written* in the sense that they are pre-composed, with often meticulous attention given to the ordering of words and vocal sound within a framework of musical and linguistic constraints.

At the same time, however, songs typically have a lower lexical density than written texts and are, prima facie, closer in register to speech, though they contain fewer discourse markers or interjections (Summer, 2018). Murphey's (1991) corpus analysis revealed song discourse to be simple, repetitive, and conversation-like, but slower than normal speech. In these respects, songs sit ambiguously on the spoken–written continuum (Summer, 2018; Trotter, 2018). In a language teaching context, researchers have explored how the oral–aural nature of recorded songs holds potential for teaching speaking and listening (e.g., Ludke, Ferreira, and Overy, 2014; Murphey, 1990), and the slower and more repetitive nature of songs as identified by Murphey (1991) is arguably advantageous in this regard, particularly at less advanced stages of language learning. There is also some evidence to suggest that listening to songs stimulates subvocal articulations – unvoiced, 'inner monologue[s] that engage motor mechanisms involved in speech production' (Killingly, Lacherez, and Meuter, 2021; see Section 3.1). Meanwhile, active singing and chanting have been shown to support accuracy and confidence in speech production among language learners (e.g., Kung, 2013; Ludke, 2010; Ludke and Morgan, 2022; Mobbs and Cuyul, 2018). However, there are risks to overestimating songs' proximity to speech, and teachers should be conscious of the ways in which song texts diverge from the rules governing naturally occurring speech.

Firstly, let us consider phonology. In creating a song, a songwriter must negotiate a compromise between musical and linguistic systems, each of which vies for control. In the context of a song, the linguistic system, known as *prosody*, can be subdivided into the rules governing the pronunciation, rhythm, and intonation of naturalistic speech, and the stylistic conventions that govern the poetic patterning of linguistic sound in poetry. These musical and linguistic systems entail the segmentation of time into units of different length and stress emphasis, in accordance with the governing rules and conventions. Because of the referential nature of language, there are limits to how much its rules can be broken before accurate communication (of specific meanings) is compromised. In terms of phonology, this requires that the shaping of words through consonant and vowel sounds, the stress applied to syllables, and so on, must be close *enough* to speech for words to be understood as such. Similarly, the ordering of words within a line should be metrically close *enough* to speech to be intelligible (i.e., recognised and processed by the brain) as language. Musical notes, on the other hand, have no referential meaning in isolation; rather, they need to be arranged into structures that correspond to musical expectations (whether through fulfilment or violation) and fit within the formal regularities of the musical whole, such as time signature, tempo, melody, and harmony. The notes attached to words should therefore be arranged in a way that is rhythmical and melodic *enough* to be recognised as music.

The songwriter must determine what constitutes *enough* of each element. When placed into interaction, each of these rule systems suppresses aspects of the others, requiring the songwriter to make compromises. The negotiation of linguistic and musical constraints can result in weak syllables paired with strong beats, the insertion of non-lexical vocables or silences, or the stretching or truncating of syllables to make lyrics scan better. Furthermore, rhythmic and melodic constraints can alter suprasegmental linguistic features such as duration, pitch, and tone, which in natural speech and oral poetry can signal emotional states, utterance types (e.g., questions, answers, and statements), and other subtle meanings such as sarcasm that are not implicit in grammar or lexis. Finally, whereas semi-vowels, glides, and semi-consonants such as 'r', 'w', and 'y' signal syllable boundaries in speech and oral poetry, songwriters commonly use them to align stretched syllables with the song's rhythm and melody.

A final issue relating to song's relationship to speech concerns grammar. Many researchers and practitioners have discussed songs' utility in teaching aspects of grammar, though few have done so from a robust empirical perspective. Aniuranti (2021) noted that songs can be effective in teaching English tenses to Indonesian learners. Tomczak and Lew (2019) suggested that songs can introduce students to 'multi-word units', supporting better idiomaticity in speaking and thereby 'bringing them closer to the native speaker norm' (p. 16). Akbary, Shahriari, and Hosseini Fatemi (2018) argued that songs can be particularly useful in teaching phrasal verbs. Saricoban and Metin (2000) proposed that songs can be used as an engaging entry point into grammar points, 'leading the students into a discussion [wherein] the grammar point could be practiced orally and, in a way, naturally' (n.p.). Yarmakeev and colleagues (2016) highlighted the value of repeated listening for embedding grammatical understanding, supporting both receptive and productive knowledge. Among few robust empirical studies, Busse and colleagues (2021) found that primary school learners who were taught grammar through singing outperformed those who spoke the lyrics or learnt new vocabulary through regular lessons (the control group). Ludke's (2018) study found that students whose lessons incorporated song-related activities outperformed those whose lessons incorporated visual art and drama, including on grammar tasks.

Despite the lack of empirical evidence, the largely practitioner-authored literature indicates that educators find songs to be a versatile and engaging tool for teaching grammar. It is important to note, however, that songs do not always adhere to the rules that govern standard language usage. Trotta (2018, p. 27) asserted that popular music songs commonly feature 'structures considered ungrammatical or infelicitous in ordinary speech, but which are normal in their context'. Summer (2018) and others observed that ungrammatical constructions have become idiomatic in many forms of popular music. Finally, there can be a tension between British and American English in English pop songs (Summer, 2018), reflecting the two historical and still dominant centres of popular music production.

Reflecting the widespread tacit belief among educators that ELT songs are (or should be) proximal to speech, we have found that clients, reviewers, and other stakeholders can be uneasy about features such as stretched syllables, melisma, or non-lexical vocables, believing them to undermine the clarity, prominence, and authenticity of the target language and therefore to present unnecessary barriers to students' apprehension and understanding. Yet, as we have discussed in this section, although songs can display many features common to ordinary speech and have been used effectively to teach pronunciation, listening, lexis, and even grammar, there are reasons to be cautious in assuming a straightforward derivation or likeness. Furthermore, non-speechlike features can be vital for achieving musically successful melodies that engage learners, which, as discussed in Section 2.4, has been shown to manifest in positive learning environments that are conducive to language learning.

2.6 Conclusion

In Section 2, we have defined and unpacked several inherent features of songs that are pertinent to the use and composition of songs for language learning – the interaction of musical and linguistic systems of form and function, songs' emotional impact, the auditory and semantic implications of recorded songs, and the similarities and differences between song and speech. In Section 3, we turn to examine the features that characterise and distinguish ELT songs as a *specific type of* song, all of which derive from the intersecting historical contexts out of which the genre has emerged.

3 Contextualising ELT Songs

In this section we situate ELT songs in relation to the contexts from which they emerged and where they circulate. In particular, we will look at recorded popular music, children's music, the language classroom, and the global ELT publishing industry.

3.1 ELT Songs as Popular Music

As noted in Section 2.3, most songs used in the language classroom, including ELT songs, are recorded pop songs. They therefore display lyrical, musical, and sonic features that derive from the historical development of record production. Let us now look more closely then at the historical emergence and development of popular music, the consolidation of pop music as its pre-eminent and ubiquitous genre, and the characteristics of pop songs that have become normative.

In its broadest sense, the term *popular music* might simply denote any music that is valued and enjoyed by a large number of people. However, the term is usually understood to refer to a range of genres that emerged from the late nineteenth century onwards and were accessible to large audiences through the sale of sheet music and later recordings, and whose formal and aesthetic characteristics were heavily shaped by the dynamics of demand and supply and the physical constraints of media formats. Songs written for ELT use display foundational traits of popular music that can be traced back to these beginnings, including formulaic structures, simple melodies, and humorous, topical, and/or sentimental, but ultimately *memorable* lyrics. These features are also central to songs' appeal and pedagogical utility in the language classroom.

Popular music is often associated with 'ordinary' people (i.e., the populus) as distinct from social elites. In this regard, popular songs are inclusive texts that do not require any particular specialist training to enjoy or understand. However, genres of popular music are also associated with identity groups defined according to age, race, gender, class, and ethnicity. As we discuss in more detail in Section 3.2, popular music is also a key developmental resource (Herbert and Dibben, 2018) through which young people construct their identities, align themselves with different groups, and distance themselves from other groups. As discussed in Section 2.3, social identities can be signified in songs by way of sonic markers, and playing popular music in a social setting such as a classroom might therefore draw attention to, and/or potentially marginalise, different group identities. Songs' potential for both inclusion *and exclusion* must therefore be given due attention in the use and composition of ELT songs.

3.1.1 ELT Songs as Pop Songs

Although 'pop' is simply an abbreviation of 'popular', 'pop music' usually refers to a genre of music that emerged after the Second World War, principally in the USA but also in the UK and elsewhere. Like other forms of popular music that preceded it, pop music featured musical aesthetics, lyrical preoccupations, and formal characteristics that resulted from the convergence of particular technological, economic, social, and political developments. In particular, pop music emerged alongside the notion of the teenager, a term that referred to post-war adolescents with abundant leisure time, lenient parents, and disposable income, who would become pop music's core market. Early pop song lyrics were often vignettes of teenage settings such as parties and dances, with themes of romance, friendship, new fashions and trends, and the killjoy tendencies of adult authority figures. Musically, early Anglo-American pop music was heavily derivative of African American styles such as blues, jazz, rhythm and blues, and rock and roll. It typically featured a backbeat played on a drum kit, a substructure of electric bass guitar, electric guitar, and other amplified instruments, prominent vocals, and the creative use of recording technology to achieve new sounds and sonic environments (see Section 2.3). Pop songs' structural norms were also determined by limitations on length imposed by the runtime of seven-inch 45rpm records, and by radio programming. A typical length of between two-and-a-half and three minutes emerged from the 1950s.

Owing to the market-driven pursuit of novelty, constant innovation is also a defining feature of pop music. The proliferation of genres such as rock, metal, hip-hop, and electronic dance music (EDM) (and myriad subgenres thereof) reflects attempts to codify these innovations and mark their social and political origins. However, pop music's foundational musical and lyrical traits – short song lengths, formulaic structures, backbeat, prominent vocals, and youth themes – are common denominators across most pop genres.

As mass products, pop songs have to be memorable to secure listeners' attention and compel people to buy them. This is achieved through 'hooks' – melodic, rhythmic, or lyrical 'moments of salient appeal' (Smith, 2009, p. 311). The sequencing of hooks occurs at various levels within a pop song's arrangement. For example, a guitar riff might recur every two bars throughout an eight-bar verse, while a chord sequence might recur every four bars and a vocal phrase might last a full eight bars. Each of these hooks is an opportunity to lodge the song in the listener's memory. Over time, mainstream pop songs have become 'hook-laden' – crammed full of hooks to maximise the chance of commercial success. In ELT songs, appealing hooks can promote learner engagement, and if memorable may also directly support language acquisition.

3.1.2 Earworms

Catchy hooks can stimulate 'the spontaneous recall and repeating of a tune in one's mind' (Jakubowski et al., 2017, p. 122). This phenomenon is referred to as involuntary musical imagery (INMI) but is commonly known by another metaphorically invasive name: *earworms*.⁵ Despite popular belief that earworms are unwanted intrusions (Beaman, 2018; Beaman and Williams, 2010), research has suggested that enjoyment is an important factor in the establishment of earworms (Arthur, 2023; Liikkanen and Jakubowski, 2020). Enjoyment of a song is more likely to drive repeated listening or induce singing, both of which facilitate repeated exposure to earworms and constitute forms of rehearsal. While singing involves the physical production of sound, earworms also derive from a compulsion 'to continually rehearse the line in working memory' (Killingly et al., 2021, p. 458). This is a form of 'subvocal articulation' that activates our phonological loop, 'a crucial component in maintaining verbal and other auditory information in memory and facilitating the passage of information from short to long-term memory' (Arthur, 2023, p. 8). Murphey (1990) first proposed a link between earworms – the 'song-stuck-in-my-head phenomenon' (p. 53) – and Krashen's (1983) concept of *din* – the involuntary rehearsal of language as a consequence of the language acquisition device (LAD) being stimulated. Murphey (1990) hypothesised that, in an ELT context, 'sticky' songs may support recall of phrases and lexis. While the link between earworms and L2 acquisition remains under-explored and unresolved empirically, it is (to us at least!) intuitively persuasive.

Research reviewed by Killingly and colleagues (2021) suggested that earworms are easy to sing and feature simplistic and repetitious melodies, notes that are longer in length and closer in pitch, fast tempos, and 'melodic contours characteristic of Western music' (p. 457). Liikkanen and Jakubowski's (2020) review found that inclusion of lyrics and 'locus around the chorus' (p. 1209), in addition to those factors identified by Killingly and colleagues (2021), was common across experiences of INMI. Beaman's (2018) finding that lyrical music (i.e., songs) induced nearly 50 per cent more earworms than instrumental music lends weight to the proposition that the pairing of music and language results in more memorable hooks, while findings related to singability and melodic shape (e.g., Killingly et al., 2021) offer insight into the possible characteristics of hooky vocal lines. As ELT songwriters, we often strive to pair catchy, aphoristic lyrics with hooky melodies, and our conviction that this will embed our songs in listeners' heads is rooted in our having experienced, like most people, the earworm phenomenon ourselves. That songs in foreign languages appear to induce as many earworms as those in listeners' native language (see Arthur, 2023; Liikkanen, 2012) lends weight to their potential facility in L2 teaching.

---

⁵ Some scholars consider earworms to be a subset of, rather than synonymous with, INMI (e.g., Arthur, 2023; Beaman, 2018).

It is particularly striking that the prevailing characteristics of pop(ular) songs – their simplicity, their easy singability and listenability, their formulaic structures, their repetitiveness, their regular rhythms, and their being memorable to the point of inducing earworms – often seen as evidence of their being 'banal, homogeneous, unsophisticated, undiscerning, uncultured, low, inauthentic, fake, commercial, conservative, unimaginative, conformist or just plain stupid' (Huber, 2013, p. 8), are among the reasons cited by language teachers for using songs (see, e.g., Engh, 2013; Tegge, 2018). Indeed, there appears to be clear alignment between the features that pop songwriters incorporate into songs in pursuit of commercial success and the pedagogical affordances of songs in the language classroom.

3.1.3 Deixis

A final salient dimension of ELT songs' status as pop songs concerns the role of the listener as a meaning-making subject. In Section 2, we discussed how songs generate meaning through the interplay of their lyrical, musical, and sonic aspects. A further dimension of meaning-making ascribed to popular music is the extent to which listeners project their own experiences onto – or perceive their own experiences *in* – pop songs (Frith, 1989; Moore, 2016). This results in part from pop songs' often oblique lyrics, and in particular their vagueness in terms of time, space, and the identity of the protagonist (Summer, 2018). Tlili (2016) examined the use of *deictic* words (e.g., you, me, here, there, now, then) in high-charting songs in the UK to establish relational and spatio-temporal contexts that appeal to target audiences. Tlili (2016) found that first- and second-person deictic expressions (e.g., 'I wish you were here' / 'when will I see you again?') were used to project the 'personhood' of, and 'establish and maintain rapport with', listeners (p. 234). Spatio-temporal context meanwhile was kept vague through the deictic words 'here' and 'now', such that 'each member of the audience can identify with the content of these lines wherever s/he happens to be' (Tlili, 2016, p. 235). Thus, pop songs' lack of rational, spatial, and temporal precision invites the listener to 'appropriate [songs] as their own, interpret them individually, and place them into their own context' (Summer, 2018, p. 194). However, because ELT songs are usually written to a linguistic brief centring on specific lexis or grammar, incorporating vagueness can be challenging. We explore this challenge in Section 5.

3.2 ELT Songs: A Subgenre of Children's Music

Typically, ELT songs are written for school-aged children and as such are a subgenre of children's music. Despite its ubiquity and commercial profitability, children's music, Vinge (2017) notes, is 'seldom the subject of criticism in musical press or media' (p. 1). It is also under-represented in academic research on education (Maloy, 2018; Vestad, 2017), musicology (Vinge, 2017), children's media entertainment (Smith, 2010), and broadcasting (Deaville, 2011). This is perhaps an indication that, despite its prominence in children's life-worlds, children's music is not taken seriously by adults.

The development of children's music as a recorded and broadcast medium runs parallel to that of recorded music and broadcasting at large. Some of the first musical recordings were of children's songs, and the marketing of phonograph recordings for (and to) children began as early as the 1910s. These early 'juvenile records' featured stories, jokes, and sketches, replete with sound effects and animal mimicry (Smith, 2010). The earliest known examples are the phonographs of traditional verses that accompanied Ralph Mayhew's Bubble Books (1917). Bubble Books were marketed to mothers as educational resources that were vital to their children's cognitive, emotional, and cultural development, and as a form of childcare that would free up their time (Smith, 2010).

Early children's phonographs were also marketed to schools as resources for teaching music appreciation, which emerged in the early 1900s as a means to train children to actively listen to music and develop aesthetic discernment (Smith, 2010). Music appreciation classes involved children listening to music collectively under the close supervision of a teacher. Children's phonographs were thus at the vanguard of active listening pedagogies and the positioning, by adults, of recorded music within children's life-worlds. In these early mediated encounters between children and recorded sound, we can thus see the beginnings of pedagogical listening practices that would become normative and that endure today, perhaps most prominently in language education.[6]

These early developments in recorded children's music occurred in parallel with the emergence of children's broadcasting (Bignell, 2017). In the UK, children's programming emerged within months of the first BBC (British Broadcasting Corporation) radio broadcasts in 1922 and had a didactic agenda from the outset. A normative, hierarchical model emerged of authoritative 'aunts and uncles' training 'innocent but wayward' children in listening as an 'active mode of attention' (Bignell, 2017, p. 3). Thus, like children's phonographs, children's broadcasting was instrumental in constructing the ideal child listener as disciplined, quiet, and still.

Many of the foundational pedagogies, principles, and assumptions associated with songs in the language classroom, particularly the notion of active listening

---

[6] Lesson plans accompanying our songs illustrate this point (see, e.g., *The Magic Cat* (Creative Listening, 2018)). There is no space in this short Element for a substantial discussion of approaches to teaching using songs, but for existing studies see Bokiev and Ismail (2021), Coyle and Gómez Gracia (2014), Engh (2013), Kumar et al. (2022), and Tegge (2018).

and the expectation of calm and disciplined child listeners, bear the trace of these early developments. This traditional conception of active listening is, however, paradoxical in two respects. Firstly, the activity it entails – sitting quietly and still – is distinctly *passive,* while actions such as spontaneous dancing, which are indicators of emotional responsiveness to music (see Section 2.4), are implicitly discouraged. Secondly, while the traditional active listener construct conceives of musical listening as a purposeful activity, the child listener's exposure to music is prescribed and mediated by adults, and they are passive in relation to song selection. Although classroom teaching is today much more accommodating of children's physicality and spontaneity, and children are involved more actively in the selection of music, tensions arising from these paradoxes continue to influence the creation and use of songs for children.

In the decades that followed, children's music became embedded across popular culture. Notably, Disney incorporated songs into its films from *Snow White and the Seven Dwarves* (1937) onwards, marking the beginning of the animated musical format. Children's music thus became a serious business, and Disney's success in commercialising children's development paved the way for later, more overtly educational franchises such as *Sesame Street* (1971–). An ideological schism emerged in the late 1960s between the consumer-driven media culture of the USA and the paternalism of UK broadcasting. The importing of US children's shows such as *The Jackson Five* (1971) and *The Osmonds* (1972) to the UK in the early 1970s generated anxieties about consumerism, cultural imperialism, and the loss of childhood innocence, all associated with Americanisation (Bignell, 2017). Michael Jackson and Donny Osmond also spearheaded a new trend of using child or teen protagonists whose songs often featured adult-themed lyrics that simultaneously emphasised the protagonists' innocence and hinted at alluring adult futures they did not fully understand. Similarly, the music juxtaposed the arrangements and production values of mainstream adult music with conspicuously juvenile vocals (Bignell, 2017). Occupying a liminal space between childhood and adulthood has become a common trope of modern children's music (Askerøi, 2017), and the question of age-(in)appropriateness is a recurring source of tension among different stakeholders in our work as ELT songwriters.

3.2.1 Age-Appropriateness

In the late twentieth century, 'traditional children's repertoire ... was largely replaced by pop music for kids' (Vestad and Dyndahl, 2020, p. 66). Vestad and Dyndahl (2020) associated this with pop-rock aesthetics losing their association with a particular generation and instead becoming a common intergenerational frame through which 'groups around the world share their aesthetic perceptions, expressive forms and cultural practices' (pp. 71–72). However, this has also entailed a blurring of the boundaries between childhood and adulthood, with both young and old gravitating towards the extended cultural adolescence implicit in the Western pop-rock idiom. While children's fascination with cultural products intended for older consumers has long been observed (see, e.g., Baker, 2001), anxieties concerning age-appropriateness are amplified in today's highly accessible and fast-moving cultural landscape in which children are 'youthified' younger (Askerøi, 2017). This has led to growing interest in the role that music plays in children's socialisation and identity formation, and in how to balance protecting children from the dangers and moral hazards of popular music, facilitating supervised engagement with music as a developmental resource (Herbert and Dibben, 2018), allowing children to develop their own tastes and identities through choice, and introducing them to diverse cultural experiences beyond the mainstream, such as different forms of music (Faure-Carvallo, Gustems-Carnicer, and Guaus Termens, 2022; Trinick, 2012).

Educators and education researchers in particular have sought ways to harness children's enthusiasm for popular music to drive classroom engagement and to formulate curricula that resonate with children's lives and tastes (e.g., Green, 2017; Ho, 2017; Ho and Law, 2009; Kruse, 2016; Wright, 2011). Inevitably, this has centred overwhelmingly on the music classroom, but the same themes and dilemmas are pertinent to the use of music in the language classroom. In particular, the ways in which children and adolescents relate to and engage with music at different stages of their development have clear implications for how and which music is used in the language classroom. Yet relatively little attention has been given to issues of age-appropriateness in the research and scholarship surrounding song use in L2 teaching.

3.2.2 Taste and Identity

Research has shown that younger children lack genre literacy and, like older adults, are more receptive to a wider range of music than adolescents (Maloy, 2018; Vinge, 2017). Their encounters with music are heavily curated by adults, particularly parents and teachers. Around the age of ten or eleven, however, processes of socialisation and acculturation lead to a narrowing of tastes, and by the age of thirteen most young people have defined listening styles (Herbert and Dibben, 2018). Although their tastes are narrower, however, adolescents listen to more music than people at any other life stage and their reported passion for music is higher (Bonneville-Roussy et al., 2013).

Adolescents' taste development and listening practices are wholly bound up with social identity formation. During adolescence, young people build strong friendship groups, may experience early romantic relationships, and can develop affiliations with subcultures and even political movements. They begin to identify with others' characteristics, distinguish their own, and integrate these characteristics into new identities (Lamont and Hargreaves, 2019). Music preferences serve as means through which adolescents explore their identities and express them outwardly to others. As well as performing an emerging sense of individual identity, musical preferences also signal membership of in-groups and, by corollary, non-membership of out-groups – adolescents' strong preferences are accompanied by a strong dislike of other styles (Maloy, 2018).

We might reasonably assume therefore that young language learners' tolerance for stylistic difference in educational songs will differ according to age, and that, among young adolescent learners, songs could potentially provoke strong feelings of dislike or prove divisive. However, there is little research concerning the relationship between young people's music preferences and their receptiveness to specifically *educational* songs; pedagogically intentional music such as ELT songs may not be perceived by adolescents as relevant or important to their identities, and therefore not carry the same social stakes. Though it is beyond the scope of this Element, adolescents' tolerance for pedagogically intentional songs, and the salience of style and genre, would be a valuable area for future empirical work. Most important to note here is that, in our experience, anxieties surrounding adolescents' tastes, and the implications thereof for classroom engagement, figure prominently in the commissioning, composition, and production of ELT songs. However, these can be layered onto often contradictory anxieties concerning the age-appropriateness of certain styles, genres, or tropes, and whether songs are childlike enough or too grown-up. Judgements in this regard are highly subjective (see Section 4), and in the sharing, contesting, and reconciling of such judgements among stakeholders (including publishers, curriculum authors, teachers, and composers), a discursive space is established in which the normative aesthetics of the ELT song genre are shaped.

3.3 ELT Songs as an Industry Commodity

So far in this section we have situated ELT songs in relation to two overlapping musical categories, popular music and children's music. We have explored the economic, technological, and political dimensions of these categories and the market dynamics that have shaped (and continue to shape) their formal and aesthetic norms and, by extension, those of ELT songs. However, while ELT songs derive from and belong to those categories in terms of form and aesthetics, the industry context and the political economy within which ELT songs circulate are distinct from the mainstream music and entertainment industries. In this section, therefore, we situate ELT songs within the global ELT industry, a multi-billion-dollar marketplace whose principal commodity is the English language. Although lower in profile than the music and entertainment industries, the ELT industry is arguably at least as important to Anglosphere countries' strategies for achieving cultural influence and economic advantage globally. The market dynamics and ideological discourses of the ELT industry frame the commissioning of ELT songs and, consequently, influence their composition.

The 'ELT industry' is a vast domain, comprising a core of examination and certification providers, language schools, colleges, higher education providers, and coursebook and materials publishers, and a peripheral ecology of websites and apps, trade publications, tech start-ups, freelance tutors, and other content creators and service providers. Estimating the total revenue or market size of the industry is therefore challenging; estimates vary depending on how the industry is delimited. Nonetheless, estimates all affirm the industry's multi-billion-dollar status. In 2016, Pearson (one of the industry's largest companies) estimated the global ELT industry's annual turnover to be US$194 billion (Jordan and Gray, 2019), while 2023 reports estimated a global ELT market size of US$66.5 billion (Market Growth Reports, 2023).

Increasingly, ELT start-ups and independent content creators are exploiting new media and technologies to reach global audiences of teachers, parents, and, of course, children. This new media landscape is challenging the established products and norms of the industry's dominant players, but it also presents opportunities for creative entrepreneurs. Perhaps the most prominent example of recent years is Planet Pop ELT Songs, a UK-based start-up that streams its songs over YouTube and Spotify and monetises accompanying lesson plans and other resources via a tiered subscription model. Planet Pop targeted a valuation of £100 million in 2022 (Godding, 2021) and secured backing from Sony Music Publishing in 2024.

The UK has an approximately 30 per cent market share of the global ELT industry (LearnCube, 2023), the second largest after the USA's. Its leading position has been actively pursued by the state via the British Council, a non-departmental public body established in 1934 to promote British culture, goods, and services globally. In the era of the British Council, the English language transitioned from being the lingua franca of an atrophying empire to the UK's second largest export commodity after North Sea oil (Mackenzie, 2021). Publishers of ELT materials are a major segment of the ELT industry, whose main products are coursebooks targeted at all education levels from kindergarten to postgraduate. Here, the UK is pre-eminent; UK publishers sold 58.7 million coursebook units in 2019 (Publishers Association, 2019) and leading coursebooks such as those in Oxford University Press's Headway series have sold in excess of 70 million units (Ożóg, 2018, cited in Mishan, 2022).

Despite new media innovations and disruptions, coursebooks remain the dominant paradigm for ELT globally, to the extent that their suitability is rarely questioned by educators (Akbari, 2008; Jordan and Gray, 2019). However, coursebooks have been critiqued in academic research both for the pedagogical structures they prescribe (Jordan and Gray, 2019) and for their ideological assumptions and role in perpetuating linguistic and cultural imperialism (e.g., Al Hosni, 2015; Budairi, 2018; R'boul, 2022). In particular, scholars have suggested that ELT coursebooks promote capitalism and neoliberalism through the foregrounding of 'cultural authorities, norms, and values that the United States and other countries where English is spoken as a first language accept and acknowledge' (Grant and Wong, 2018, p. 2; see also, e.g., R'boul, 2022). Others have discussed coursebooks' perpetuation of ethnic stereotypes (e.g., Bouzid, 2016), gender stereotypes (e.g., Tyarakanita et al., 2021), and Western-centric ideals of citizenship (e.g., Shi and Lim, 2022). Others still have highlighted their role in upholding varieties of 'standard English' considered 'native' to the UK and other 'Inner Circle' countries and spoken predominantly by the white middle classes. Some have argued that this marginalises international speakers (see, e.g., Nizamani and Shah, 2022), 'misrepresents … the sociolinguistic reality of Britain with its numbers of "superdiverse" cities' (Mishan, 2022, p. 499), and 'ignores evidence that indicates that even monolingual mother tongue speakers of English speak … dialects that may or may not reflect the usage prescribed through "standard" English' (Mahboob, 2011, p. 49). Importantly, some studies noted that listening material still overwhelmingly features 'received pronunciation' and other native speaker accents (e.g., Buckledee, 2010; Chan, 2019; Mishan, 2022), even in locally published or local-market-specific coursebooks (Chan, 2019; Nguyen, Marlina, and Cao, 2020).

While songs have featured in ELT coursebooks for decades, their presence has significantly increased alongside the digitisation of coursebook materials. Songs are sometimes included in the student coursebook as core texts, but they can also be included as supplementary texts in accompanying teacher's books or digital learning platforms. Songs are used for a variety of pedagogical purposes, including arousing learners' interest, improving pronunciation, teaching vocabulary and grammar, helping with understanding of sentence structure, and fostering intercultural awareness, though researchers have identified different levels of emphasis between publishers and between publishing countries (see, e.g., Peng, Shi, and Zhang, 2023).

Many of our ELT songs were commissioned for inclusion in coursebooks and incorporate lexis and grammar that correspond to particular coursebook units. As songwriters, we do not participate in high-level decision-making about the sociolinguistic diversity of coursebook syllabi. However, issues relating to the representation of sociolinguistic and cultural diversity nonetheless emerge in writing, text-setting, and recording, particularly in relation to national and regional accents and the use of British English versus American English. At the level of genre, the expectations of standard, 'correct' English can be at odds with markers of identity in popular music, particularly through vernacular language and through the singer's voice, as touched upon previously in Sections 2.3, 2.5, and 3.1. While the briefs we receive often demonstrate a concern for cultural and even sociolinguistic diversity, the belief that 'songs [for] English learners must have proper grammar instead of grammatical errors' (Ramadhania, 2022, p. 82) is deeply entrenched, precluding the use of non-standard Englishes and thus of one of pop music's common compositional traits.

The ideological dimension of coursebooks is also significant. As Mishan (2022) noted, coursebooks are 'de facto cultural artefact[s]' (p. 492) whose vignettes, characters, themes, and activities enshrine particular values. This has been critiqued in terms of cultural imperialism, hegemony, and erasure (e.g., Mishan, 2022; Pennycook, 2007; Ping, 2018; R'boul, 2022). However, Mishan (2022) highlighted the impossibility of cultural neutrality and thus the inevitability of coursebooks having ideological orientations. This presents a conundrum in the context of 'global' coursebooks written for multiple international markets, and for the notion of global English, which conceives of English language as an international asset untethered from, and no longer subordinate to, the Anglosphere 'Inner Circle'. Attempts to stay within safe, 'culturally universal' terrain and avoid topics or portrayals that may offend constituents of the international market[7] can result in bland, unengaging coursebooks that still betray Western values, norms, and assumptions (McCarthy, 2021). Mishan (2022) highlighted in particular the challenge of portraying family life and gender relationships in acceptable ways to markets characterised by gender segregation and strict gender roles. Publishers have attempted to mitigate these challenges by 'versioning' – publishing variations of the same coursebook for

---

[7] Mishan (2022) referred to the range of topics avoided by publishers, namely, politics, alcohol, religion, sex, narcotics, '-isms', and pork, which make up the industry acronym 'PARSNIP'.

different markets – or 'taking a calculated hit in terms of global acceptability' (Mishan, 2022, p. 496).

While we have written songs for coursebook series by major ELT publishers, to date these have been for Western national, rather than global, markets, and hazards relating to cultural (in)appropriateness or perceived imperialism have been less conspicuous than they might otherwise have been. Nonetheless, songs we have written inevitably reflect ideological positions which are not held by everyone within those markets. Outside of coursebook series, we have written songs for online platforms with a global reach that advocate for climate change activism,[8] healthy eating,[9] LGBTQI+ inclusive families,[10] and other positions that correspond to a broadly Western, left-liberal consensus but are far from universally accepted moral axioms. As such, although the thematic content of our songs is determined by the briefs we follow, as ELT songwriters we are nonetheless part of an apparatus that disseminates ideological values to children.

3.4 ELT Songs as a Classroom Resource

Perhaps the most salient context in which ELT songs are situated is the ELT classroom where they are performed, and which houses the audiences who listen to them and interact with them. As such, the classroom is the principal site for two musical practices – musical language teaching and musical language learning – which provide the rationale and the demand for the practice of ELT songwriting.

As discussed in Section 3.2, the norms of active listening that emerged with children's broadcasting and phonographs, whereby adults supervised the acousmatic performance of music to focused and attentive children, have had an enduring influence on the listening pedagogies that are a mainstay of language education. Today, listening attentively to songs in order to accurately distinguish language is the basis for activities such as 'gap-fill' and arguably remains the dominant mode of listening in the language classroom (see, e.g., Lorenzutti, 2014; Tegge, 2018). Despite this, however, language teachers today use songs for various reasons and in various ways, and we need to write ELT songs that are fit for a range of purposes.

There is a sizeable and by now relatively mature scholarly literature concerning the use of songs in language teaching, comprising case studies and accounts of practice by teachers (e.g., Feng, 2016; Yung, 2023), corpus analyses (e.g., Akbary et al., 2018; Murphey, 1990; Tegge, 2017; Werner, 2012), theoretical arguments (e.g., Boothe and West, 2015; Shen, 2009), and empirical studies of

---

[8] Creative Listening, 2020a.   [9] Creative Listening, 2020c.   [10] Creative Listening, 2020d.

language acquisition, typically using quasi-experimental designs involving pre- and post-testing (e.g., Chou, 2014; Coyle and Gómez Gracia, 2014; Mannarelli and Serrano, 2022). The last, however, are underrepresented in the literature (Davis, 2017; Tegge, 2018), with the consequence that 'pedagogical reasoning, practical choices, and their implementation largely depend on instructors' rather than empirical evidence (Tegge, 2018, p. 274). Since a number of scholars have provided thorough reviews of this literature (e.g., Davis, 2017; Engh, 2013; Lee and Schreibeis, 2021; Romero, 2017), we do not attempt such a review here. Instead, we highlight some prominent justifications for using songs in language teaching which influence and shape classroom practice and in turn influence our ELT songwriting.

3.4.1 Affective Justifications

Perhaps the most common justifications for using songs in the classroom relate to songs' perceived power to induce positive emotions and the impact this has on learners' engagement. Dewaele and colleagues (2018) identified a historical neglect of positive emotions in language teaching and research, leading to 'classes [that] are too often emotionally uninteresting or emotion-free, which leads to routine, boredom and lack of engagement' (p. 680). They argued that positive emotions 'enhance learners' ability to notice things in the classroom environment and strengthen their awareness of language input [which], in turn, allows them to absorb the FL [foreign language]' (p. 678). Drawing on Hatfield, Cacioppo, and Rapson's (1994) concept of emotional contagion,[11] according to which humans can 'catch' emotions from others, Murphey (2009) developed the concept of *linguistic contagion*. He argued that language use is another subset of human behaviour which, like emotions, is contagious and which also overlaps with emotions because language 'involves and expresses emotions at the same time' (Murphey, 2009, p. 131).

Accordingly, 'fostering a positive emotional atmosphere [to] create linguistic contagion where everyone is caught in the FL use' (Dewaele et al., 2018, p. 680) is a key task of language teachers. As discussed in Section 2.4, music has a primordial function in emotional communication and can support group cohesion. Unsurprisingly, therefore, songs are widely used to induce positive emotions and engender inclusive classroom environments that are conducive to learning. Furthermore, it has been argued that songs reduce learners' anxiety and stress (Lee and Schreibeis, 2021; Summer, 2018). A number of researchers have discussed this in relation to Krashen's (1982) affective filter hypothesis,

---

[11] Juslin and Västfjäll (2008) also discuss emotional contagion in the context of music listening – see Section 2.4.

according to which negative emotions constitute a barrier to learning that songs can help to reduce (e.g., Dolean, 2016; Engh, 2013; Lieb, 2005).

These insights and propositions from research mirror a widespread belief among language teachers that songs can engender positive classroom atmospheres (Almutairi and Shukri, 2016; Bokiev and Ismail, 2021; Tegge, 2018). In our experience, there is a common assumption that the songs most likely to lead to a positive atmosphere are 'happy' songs. In the pop idiom, happy songs are associated with characteristics such as major chords (see, e.g., Bonshor, 2023; Gagnon & Peretz, 2003; Kolchinsky et al., 2017), fast tempos (Bhat et al., 2014), danceability or 'groove' (see, e.g., Janata, Tomic and Haberman, 2012), bright timbres (Bhat et al., 2014; Bonshor, 2023), and positive lyrical themes. However, because there are several mechanisms by which music induces valenced emotions (see Section 2.4), these intrinsic features alone do not guarantee a positive emotional response. Furthermore, as discussed in Section 3.2, adolescents can be engaged by music that corresponds to their emerging sense of identity and volatile emotionality, which may include 'sad' songs. We have encountered disagreements among stakeholders concerning the emotional appropriateness of songs and take these factors into account when writing songs for different age groups.

Motivation is also linked to positive emotions. Notwithstanding differences among individual learners, research suggests that using songs in the language classroom can increase motivation and engagement (Ajibade and Ndububa, 2008; Engh, 2013; Fernández de Cañete García et al., 2022; Kumar et al., 2022; Lee and Schreibeis, 2021; Summer, 2018). However, very little explicit, comparative consideration has been given to what *types* of song, or what intrinsic characteristics of songs, increase motivation. Insights concerning children's and adolescents' tastes and listening practices, discussed in Section 3.2, might therefore offer the best basis for inferring which songs are likely to engage young learners emotionally and thereby increase their motivation.

3.4.2 The Conundrum of (In)authenticity in ELT Songs

Some researchers have proposed pop songs' authenticity as a key motivating factor (e.g., Lee and Schreibeis, 2021). A common justification among teachers for using pop songs in the classroom is that they are authentic products of the target culture that can help connect classroom activities to young people's out-of-class listening and develop their intercultural awareness (Engh, 2013; Fernández de Cañete García et al., 2022; Lee and Schreibeis, 2021; Mannarelli and Serrano, 2022; Summer, 2018; Tegge, 2018; Westphal, 2021). However, this relates to 'real' pop songs rather than ELT songs, which, despite their widespread presence in coursebooks, are almost entirely neglected in the literature and present something of a paradox. On the one hand, ELT songs possess the defining features of pop songs (see Section 3.1.1) and are thus 'real' in one sense. In accommodating pedagogical and linguistic requirements, they provide an accessible means by which learners can access, experience, and develop the skills to understand pop songs. On the other hand, as texts written specifically for the language classroom, ELT songs lack the authenticity of 'real' songs. For ELT songwriters, this paradox manifests as a compositional challenge; our task is to reconcile the competing priorities of incorporating target language and rendering it accessible to learners, while simultaneously achieving an aesthetic close to that of 'real' songs to meet young learners' expectations.

3.4.3 Language Acquisition

While all language pedagogy is ultimately oriented towards language acquisition, song use is often justified in relation to the acquisition of specific aspects of language or the development of particular language skills, whether receptive (such as listening discrimination or comprehension) or productive (such as speaking or writing). Saricoban and Metin (2000) asserted that songs can enhance learners' performance in all four skills areas – listening, writing, speaking, and reading – while others have emphasised songs' value in relation to listening and speaking in particular (e.g., Kumar et al., 2022). Tomczak and Lew (2019) proposed that songs are useful for teaching multi-word units, such as phrasal verbs and idioms, because song lyrics often contain high numbers of formulaic expressions (see also Tegge, 2017). Others have highlighted the value of songs in teaching pronunciation, whether in terms of exposure to 'native' accents (e.g., Shen, 2009) or simply in terms of being comprehensible (Saldiraner and Cinkara, 2021). As discussed in Section 2.5, others have focused on songs' utility in teaching grammar (e.g., Aniuranti, 2021; Saricoban and Metin, 2000; Tomczak and Lew, 2019; Upendran, 2001). While the level of empirical support for these assertions varies, such beliefs shape pedagogic practice in the classroom and thus contribute to the uses, expectations, and criteria against which we write ELT songs.

3.4.4 Reasons for Not Using Songs

Despite widespread belief in the value of songs for language learning, several studies have identified a discrepancy between teachers' beliefs and their practice (e.g., Almutairi and Shukri, 2016; Bokiev and Ismail, 2021; Kumar et al., 2022; Tegge, 2018). Accordingly, some scholars have shed light on why and how teachers *do not* use songs. Such studies are particularly valuable for highlighting limitations of 'real' songs that ELT songs can surmount, as well as barriers presented by environmental or cultural factors. Teachers in Bokiev and Ismail's (2021) study cited 'lack of teaching materials', 'difficulty finding songs', 'time constraints', 'lack of facilities', 'large class sizes', and 'lack of training and peer support' as reasons for not using songs (p. 1511). Of these factors, ELT songs address at least the first two and possibly the last; they relieve the challenge of finding songs that simultaneously feature the target language, are age-appropriate, and appeal to young learners' tastes. Invariably, ELT songs are also accompanied by lesson plans, reducing the need for training.

Respondents in Tegge's (2018) study also cited cultural, political, and institutional factors, difficulty aligning songs with the prescribed curriculum, and 'fear of being out of sync with the students' (p. 282). Lending support for the value of ELT songs, Tegge (2018) called for 'more preselected songs and prefabricated materials in accordance with curricula including activities beyond the "dreaded gap-fill"' (p. 283).

Murphey (1992) listed twenty barriers to song use from the teacher's perspective. In addition to those identified by Tegge (2018) and Bokiev and Ismail (2021), Murphey (1992) noted teachers' beliefs that songs could be *too* exciting or distracting for students, often contained poor vocabulary and grammar, could include violent and sexist themes, and detracted from the core syllabus. Murphey (1992) also observed that teachers doubted their own musicality, and that both teachers and students could be reluctant to sing in class.

Murphey's work was published more than thirty years ago, and song use in the language classroom has become much more established in the interim. Nonetheless, these concerns persist and can be addressed with ELT songs. As songwriters, we work in close collaboration with materials authors to ensure that songs complement, rather than distract from, core syllabi and are fully aligned with the lexis, grammar, and skills foci of corresponding coursebook units. We can mitigate anxieties about singing by composing melodies that are easy to sing, such as stepwise melodies within the pitch range of a typical musically untrained child, or incorporating clapping and/or dance cues that provide alternative opportunities for interaction.[12]

However, one reason listed by Murphey (1992) highlights a concern specific to ELT songs: 'EFL [English as a foreign language] songs are boring' (p. 8). In our experience, this negative perception of ELT songs still endures among many teachers and publishers. Indeed, 'something that doesn't sound like an ELT

---

[12] See, e.g., Creative Listening, 2020b.

song' is a common demand from publishers, suggesting that ELT songs are associated with aesthetic features that mark them as inferior to 'real' pop songs. Historically, these included 'auto-accompaniment' backing tracks, poor recording quality, and limited textural depth and/or variation. Recent years have seen a trend towards ELT songs that mirror the prevailing aesthetics of mainstream pop music and whose production values are broadly consistent with commercial standards. However, some shortcomings that are intrinsic to songs' melodic, harmonic, and lyrical aspects, as opposed to their production, still persist. In our experience, these include:

- basic harmonic structures with an over-reliance on functional I, IV and V triads (as opposed to richer, altered or extended voicings), resulting in a lack of emotional depth;
- vocal melodies with no memorable hooks (particularly in the chorus) and featuring limited syncopation;
- lyrics with no discernible hooks, and particularly choruses that do not introduce novel elements;
- a lack of attention to instrumental arrangements.

We try to avoid these shortcomings in our own songwriting and in particular seek to shape our songs around strong melodic and lyrical hooks. However, while an awareness of the characteristics of bad ELT songs is helpful, it does not alone lead to good ELT songs. It is important to also develop an understanding of what makes ELT songs good, according to different criteria and different stakeholders.

4 Evaluating ELT Songs

Evaluative judgements are inherently subjective and therefore a matter not just of *which* criteria but of *whose* criteria (Vinge, 2017). Different stakeholders in the production, use, and reception of ELT songs hold different evaluative criteria, and listening to, negotiating, and reconciling different stakeholders' evaluative judgements is an integral aspect of ELT songwriting. In this section we draw on our extensive experience of collaborating on ELT song projects to propose the criteria according to which different stakeholders and agents evaluate the quality of ELT songs.

4.1 The Songwriter's Perspective

Vinge (2017) asserted that, for songwriters, good music is 'music that [they] themselves believe in' (p. 13). While engaged in the act of songwriting, songwriters rely on intuition and are guided by their emotional, embodied responses to the sound they are creating. What 'feels' good is deemed good and retained, and what does not is discarded. Often unarticulated evaluative judgements during the songwriting process are determined by songwriters' own tastes, their genre literacy (their familiarity with the normative traits of different genres), and their ability to produce music and/or lyrics that display genres' normative traits. Songwriters may also prioritise novelty and, conversely, seek to generate ideas that *depart from* those normative traits.

This foundational evaluative system undergirds all songwriting because a songwriter's own tastes and knowledge are always part of their referential framework. Where a song is composed for a third party and/or a specific purpose, however, this evaluative system is mediated by external criteria corresponding to stakeholders' needs and might even be *at odds* with the songwriter's own tastes. Therefore, ELT songwriters must anticipate evaluative divergence and accept the need to reconcile their own tastes and preferences with other stakeholders' requirements and expectations.

4.2 The Publisher's Perspective

Publishers' expectations correspond to songs' intended pedagogical-linguistic function within the syllabus (e.g., to teach particular phrasal verbs) and general suitability (e.g., being engaging and classroom-appropriate), but also to the standards established by previously commissioned and/or competitors' products (including those of independent creators and start-ups – see Section 3.3). Publishers also evaluate songs against criteria that are specific to the intended target markets; as discussed in Section 3.3, publishers are careful to ensure that materials are culturally appropriate and inoffensive. This is obviously pertinent to lyrics but can also extend to the musical styles and timbres used, and particularly those associated with aggression or rebellion, such as metal, punk, or hip-hop. Finally, publishers' evaluations are made through the filter of individual employees' musical tastes, or through conversation among different individuals.

In short, then, a good song from a publisher's perspective is one that fulfils its pedagogic purpose, meets or exceeds normative standards, is culturally sensitive and age-appropriate, and aligns with representatives' tastes. However, since these criteria are often tacit, and publisher representatives are often musically untrained and therefore lack the specialist vocabulary needed to describe music verbally, they are not always articulated clearly in briefs. This requires flexibility on the part of publisher and songwriter, and an iterative, back-and-forth working model that establishes a common frame of reference.

4.3 The ELT Author's Perspective

Usually, ELT coursebook authors are former teachers who have transitioned into writing after years of classroom practice and thus possess a wealth of pedagogical expertise. In addition, they possess specific expertise in relation to the composition of coursebooks, including how linguistic content is ordered, how activities are sequenced and so on, and how to reconcile their vision with the demands of publishers to ensure that the product is both pedagogically effective and commercially viable (Atkinson, 2021a, 2021b).

Historically, the ELT author's vision underpins each project, and their evaluations regarding the quality and appropriateness of songs are therefore critical. Like those of publishers and teachers, authors' preferences derive from personal tastes, memories, and values, and also correspond to songs' intended pedagogical purpose. In evaluating songs, authors will likely prioritise pedagogical but also aesthetic alignment with their vision for the project as a whole.

Further, ELT authors are credited by name in coursebooks and other materials, and therefore have reputational and commercial stakes that likely compound the importance placed on vision alignment. In our experience, this can manifest in anxieties relating to the general 'feel' of songs, but also focused concerns relating to specific instances within songs such as, for example, the melismatic text-setting of a single syllable across multiple notes (see Section 2.5). However, authors can be effusive in their feedback when they encounter a song that aligns strongly with their vision, and their enthusiasm is an important gauge of quality that helps us to iteratively shape songs in alignment with their vision and expectations.

4.4 The Teacher's Perspective

From a teacher's perspective, ELT songs are not cultural products consumed for personal enjoyment but tools for teaching children L2 knowledge and skills. Teachers are therefore likely to evaluate songs primarily in terms of their use value for themselves (i.e., the extent to which the songs enable them to accomplish a task or make that task easier) and the songs' pedagogical value for their students. The latter can be divided into 'pedagogically intentional' value relating to specific educational objectives (e.g., teaching past continuous tense) and 'pedagogically functional' value relating to a song's 'contribution through its lyrics to reflection, enlightenment, and growth' (Vinge, 2017, p. 7). A further pedagogical dimension relates to a song's potential to stimulate a positive atmosphere and thereby render learners more receptive to language (see Section 3.4.1). Teachers' evaluation of this dimension may correspond to tacit beliefs concerning age-appropriateness, emotional valence (e.g., happy versus sad), other features that each individual associates with a positive classroom environment, and observed effects in the classroom, such as whether a song causes learners to smile, laugh, dance, or sing.

Teachers acting *in loco parentis* are also likely to evaluate songs according to similar criteria to parents. Just as parents' evaluations are 'both socio-cultural and aesthetic' and derive from 'a highly complex mix of class-related taste, discourses, personal identity work, childhood memories, and consideration of their children's best interests' (Vestad and Dyndahl, 2020, pp. 66–67), so teachers' evaluations derive from the interplay of memories from childhood and professional life, tastes, prevailing discourses, and consideration of students' best interests. Teachers may perhaps be more concerned than parents with accommodating diversity to reflect and cater to the diverse classes in their charge and to mirror the diversity inherent in society (Vinge, 2017).

Teachers invited to review ELT songs during the production process do not usually test the materials in a classroom setting. Instead, they evaluate them based on their extensive prior professional experience. Like those of publishers, therefore, their evaluations are inherently comparative.

4.5 The Young Learner's Perspective

While teachers are the 'end users' of ELT songs, learners are the target *consumers*. It is therefore striking that, in our experience, young learners are rarely consulted directly as part of the commissioning, composition, and production of ELT songs. There are understandable reasons for this: firstly, eliciting actionable feedback directly from children is challenging because they can lack the analytical or expressive capacity to verbalise their preferences; and secondly, young children lack metacognitive awareness of what helps them learn and so are unable to evaluate songs pedagogically. Nonetheless, as Bickford (2019) observed in relation to children's music, evaluative standards in ELT are arguably based on 'an underlying contradiction, in which the child audiences who make this music possible must be disavowed in favor of the discernment and taste of adults' (p. 229). Bickford's (2019) observation can be extended beyond musical preference to students' learning preferences and backgrounds, which should be acknowledged and, where possible, attended to in the accompanying activities.

Given the dearth of first-hand data on children's preferences for classroom songs, teachers' observations offer crucial insight into songs' reception by young learners. Drawing on decades of experience of writing children's music, Maloy (2018) identified twenty-nine musical, lyrical, and sonic attributes that children respond to positively, whether physically, emotionally, or imaginatively. These are: 'an overall melodic range of between a fourth and an octave'; 'scale-wise melodies'; 'melodic intervals of up to a sixth'; 'a reliance on tonic, subdominant and dominant chords'; 'use of a major key'; 'no or minimal vocal harmonies'; 'perfect cadences'; 'regular common time signatures of two four, three four or four four'; 'obvious and regular rhythms'; 'high tempi'; 'AB or AAA structure'; 'brevity ... assessed as being 25 per cent or more shorter than the average hit of the year of release'; 'strong use of perfect or half rhyme'; 'high levels of metric repetition'; 'short, discrete lyrical phrases'; 'songs where the majority of the words have just one or two syllables'; 'lyrical themes of animals, rural or domestic settings'; 'visual imagery'; 'first-person narrator'; 'child protagonist'; 'obvious didactic or moral intent'; 'nonsense rhymes'; 'comedy themes'; 'vocalists who are children[,] adult females or male adult voices speeded-up to sound like a child'; 'clear diction'; 'highly enunciated vocals'; 'the use of representational sound effects'; 'high-pitched tones such as bells, glockenspiels, or xylophones'; and 'the foregrounding of the vocals in the overall mix of the recording' (Maloy, 2018, p. 35).

Most attributes identified by Maloy (2018) chime with our own observations of what makes songs appealing to children. In some cases, however, they are potentially at odds with the pedagogical and/or linguistic aims attributed to ELT songs – 'high tempi', for example, might impose a pace onto linguistic constructions that is unmanageable for the beginner language learner. Furthermore, Maloy's (2018) focus is early childhood, whereas the majority of our songs are aligned with language curricula that typically start in primary school and continue throughout secondary school.[13] As discussed in Section 3.2.2, this coincides with the periods of identity formation when young people develop strong musical preferences and an accompanying resistance to other music. Many of the attributes in Maloy's (2018) list are unlikely to appeal to (pre-)adolescents.

De Vries (2010) observed that children can develop increasingly negative attitudes towards school music during this period owing to 'the absence of connection between the cultural contexts of school, home and community when it comes to music learning and engagement' (p. 4). De Vries (2010) argued that 'to engage upper primary school children in school music[,] there needs to be an understanding of what music upper primary children prefer' (p. 4).[14] Although De Vries (2010) was writing about music education, these insights are pertinent to the use of music in language teaching and to the composition of ELT songs for use with older children and young adolescents. Adolescents' quality evaluations are likely to involve genre-based aesthetic criteria, taste discourses shared among peers, and

---

[13] According to the European Commission / EACEA / Eurydice's (2023) *Key Data on Teaching Languages at School in Europe* report, in most countries children start learning a foreign language as a compulsory component of the curriculum between the ages of six and eight.

[14] De Vries was writing in the Australian context, where upper primary refers to children of twelve to thirteen years old.

early identity work, and thus – as one might expect – resemble an emerging version of the adult evaluative processes undertaken by parents, teachers, and so on. A key challenge of ELT songwriting is that children's development (hormonal, cognitive, social, etc.) is far from synchronised, such that some children within a class may be 'older' (i.e., more mature) than others. Good ELT songs therefore need to be accessible to developmentally diverse learners.

4.6 What Is a 'Good' ELT Song? An Evaluative Framework

So far in this section we have considered the expectations, preferences, and criteria that different stakeholders hold in relation to songs, and specifically songs for use in language teaching. In this final subsection, we synthesise these considerations with insights from Sections 2 and 3 to formulate an evaluative framework for quality ELT songwriting, comprising twelve criteria and ten dilemmas.

4.6.1 Criteria for Evaluating ELT Songs

An ELT song should ...

1. Be better than competing products.
2. Be culturally appropriate in relation to the target market.
3. Be age-appropriate.
4. Appeal to young learners at different stages of development.
5. Be fit for its designated pedagogical purpose.
6. Not require training or cultural capital to enjoy.
7. Be singable and/or danceable.
8. Have coherent and predictable structures (within and across lyrics and music) in line with normative popular music formulae.
9. Feature repetition.
10. Have lyrical and musical hooks.
11. Have emotional and narrative alignment between music, lyrics, and sonics.
12. Meet the normative production standards of 'real' songs.

4.6.2 Dilemmas in ELT Songwriting

1. Speech proximity or optimal musicality?

There is a widespread belief among language educators that songs approximate – or at least *should* approximate – speech (see Section 2.5). At the same time, strong melodies are essential if songs are to be memorable and engaging. Reconciling the imperatives of musicality and speech proximity is therefore a perennial dilemma in ELT songwriting.

2. Target language only or embedded target language?

Typically, ELT songs are deliberately aligned with target language. However, writing lyrics from level-limited vocabulary can severely constrain the song's thematic and metric possibilities and make it difficult to write memorable hooks. On the other hand, incorporating language outside of the target language can impede learners' comprehension. Then again, limiting a song to target language arguably fails to prepare learners for engaging with 'real' songs. In our experience, this dilemma is usually encountered in discussions around a brief prior to the songwriting process but can be revisited at the feedback stages.

3. Standard versus non-standard English pronunciation?

The listening materials of publishers in the UK usually (though not exclusively) feature speakers with neutral British accents. However, as discussed in Section 3.3, accusations of linguistic imperialism have been levelled at coursebooks for implicitly upholding the supremacy of 'standard' English over 'world' or 'non-standard' Englishes, and researchers have highlighted the affordances of popular music for introducing other Englishes into the classroom (e.g., Westphal, 2021). These tensions can emerge during the songwriting process and vocal recording, particularly in relation to accented pronunciation.

4. Standard versus non-standard English grammar?

Closely related to Dilemma 3, this dilemma relates to whether grammatical constructions that are erroneous according to the rules of standard English(es), but that are common to non-standard Englishes and may also be prominent, authentic tropes of popular music genres, are permitted.

5. Cultural specificity or universalism?

As discussed in Section 3.3, ELT materials reflect the values and mores of the context where they are produced, which may be at odds with those of contexts where the materials are to be used. This has prompted attempts to create culturally 'universal' materials; however, these have also been criticised for being bland and uninteresting. Writing songs that are inclusive of and inoffensive to learners from diverse cultural backgrounds, but remain engaging, is therefore a key challenge of ELT songwriting.

6. Audio fidelity versus aesthetic normativity?

As discussed in Section 2.3, invented sonic environments are an expected characteristic of pop songs. However, these can differ markedly from naturalistic environments and are arguably therefore not an ideal basis for practising auditory discrimination. On the other hand, if the aim is to support young learners' engagement with 'real' songs, then ELT songs should adhere to normative standards. A dilemma thus emerges around balancing audio fidelity with normative production standards.

7. Fashionable versus future-proof?

Related to Dilemma 6, this dilemma relates to ensuring thematic, musical, and sonic contemporariness so as to align with the music that young listeners engage with beyond the classroom, while also avoiding the risk of songs sounding out of date, particularly if the coursebook and/or materials are intended to be in use for many years.

8. Childish or grown-up?

The intended audiences of ELT songs span childhood and early adolescence, during which learners will be at different stages of development and have diverse preferences and accompanying dislikes. This presents a challenge in terms of balancing child- and adolescent-oriented thematic content and aesthetics in order to produce songs that are engaging and accessible to developmentally diverse cohorts.

9. Direct specificity versus oblique deixis?

As discussed in Section 3.1.2, a key dimension of pop songs' emotional potency and consequent popularity is that they can be interpreted through the prism of listeners' own (real or imagined) experiences. Using deictic vocabulary, especially in oblique choruses, establishes spatial (e.g., 'here', 'there'), temporal (e.g., 'now', 'then'), and person ('I', 'we', 'you') deixis that place the listener at the centre and thereby invite personalised interpretations of songs. However, ELT song briefs often demand lyrics that address specific themes very directly or impose restrictions on general vocabulary (see Dilemma 2). The competing aims of directness and obliqueness, and specificity and deixis, must therefore be negotiated to ensure that the created songs are engaging and serve their linguistic purpose.

10. Activity versus passivity?

This final dilemma relates to the tension between traditional modes of active listening that demand listeners' focused attention and modes of listening wherein embodied/kinetic responses are encouraged. Just as teachers must balance focus and fun in their classrooms, ELT songwriters must ensure that an appropriate balance is struck in the composition of ELT songs. While songwriters aim to create songs that will engage learners, occasionally a song may seem *too* engaging, to the point of distraction (Murphey, 1992; see also Section 3.4.4). In our experience, this is most often owing to energy level or countercultural allure (with pop punk songs being particularly prone), and a balance can usually be achieved through adjustments to tempo and timbre.

5 Writing ELT Songs

In Section 4 we considered the needs, priorities, and expectations of different stakeholders involved in the commissioning, composition, use, and reception of ELT songs, from which we derived twelve key criteria and ten compositional dilemmas that songwriters must engage with when writing ELT songs. In this penultimate section we focus on our own songwriting practice and highlight, through examples, how these dilemmas manifest, and how we reconcile competing priorities at different stages during the songwriting process.

5.1 Responding to the Brief: From Extra-Musical Requirements to Musical Content

Our ELT songwriting projects are usually either commissioned directly by a publisher familiar with our previous work or secured through an open or invited tendering process. Once secured, each project invariably begins with a meeting attended by a publisher representative, the coursebook or materials author(s), the songwriters (us), and a project manager. The general vision for the coursebook, the strategy for and role of songs within the course, the requirements of the target market(s), and the project logistics are discussed, and loose ideas concerning the feel and general aesthetic of the coursebook and songs are shared. Over the course of this discussion, individuals may refer informally to songs they like (or do not like), share weblinks, or describe existing ELT materials. This and subsequent project meetings are crucial both for building rapport and consensus and for establishing a shared frame of reference (we discuss the collaborative dynamics in more detail in Section 6).

Shortly thereafter the publisher writes a brief in collaboration with the course author(s) and sends it to the songwriters. A large project brief (such as for a multi-song coursebook commission) typically includes a context report derived from market research about the education system (including years/grade structures, national curriculum requirements, teacher profiles), the culture, and the behaviours (e.g., pastimes, reading and listening habits) and preferences (e.g., popular music artists, computer games, etc.) of young people in the target market. It also sets out overarching requirements and expectations for the project as a whole.

The project brief also includes briefs for individual songs. Typically, a song brief includes the education level, the objectives of the unit in which the song will feature, the target language, the target skills, and the thematic ideas. Song briefs often take the form of a live online document to allow different stakeholders to add questions and feedback. Below is an example brief from a recent project whose target audience were Greek children aged seven to eight:

> Theme: Family
> Function: Consolidate vocab from Unit 3.
> Activities: Gap-fill and personal writing activities.
> Language: I like going to __ I don't like going to __ (e.g., swimming pool, market, gym, cinema, park, beach)
> Notes: Skateboarding and scooters are popular with this age group at the moment. Children in rural and island areas may not have access to specialist spaces like cinemas, so balance these out with natural spaces. Avoid consumerist or exclusive activities (esp. no shopping).

Although the brief contains no musical information, it is nonetheless an integral stage of the songwriting process because it establishes the lexical, grammatical, and thematic constraints within which the songwriters must work. The brief also explains the song's intended function and draws the songwriters' attention to the cultural norms of the market context.

The songwriters' first reading of the brief initiates the songwriting process proper. For us, this stage involves scanning the language and directions provided in the brief, seeking out any obvious lyrical hooks, rhymes, themes, or narrative devices, and waiting for our creative imaginations to furnish us with initial ideas for lyrics and melodies. As ideas start to arise, we audition them either subvocally (i.e., in our heads) or out loud, cycling through melodic ideas and discarding those that lead to dead-ends. To an outsider unfamiliar with collaborative songwriting, this initial exploratory evaluative process might appear strange; there is little reasoned verbal exchange between us as we audition fragments, and we communicate instead through nods, smiles, and other non-verbal responses, or the

Figure 1 Hook from 'What Do You Do at the Weekend?'

occasional 'yeah' or 'nah'. To songwriter readers, this is likely to resonate with their experiences of writing songs for general audiences.

For a recent project for a major publisher, we received a brief for a song to consolidate previously learnt grammar and vocab around the theme of hobbies and weekend activities. The target vocabulary comprised the question 'what do you do at the weekend?' and answers detailing various activities and pastimes (e.g., 'I play football', 'I do taekwondo', 'I visit family', 'I don't play tennis'). The range of activities was based on market research undertaken by the publisher concerning popular hobbies among children in the target market country.

The stress pattern of the question sentence 'what do you do at the weekend?', with strong syllables set against strong beats (**what** do you **do** at the **week**end?), hinted at a catchy hook, from which a melody arose through the exploratory process already detailed (see Figure 1).

Once we have momentum behind a promising idea – in this case, a lyric and melodic figure – we begin to discuss possibilities verbally and focus again on the requirements, constraints, and affordances of the brief. This is where the ELT songwriting process diverges from general songwriting where no extra-musical factors need to be considered. In the case of the present example, the metre of the line is relatively close to natural speech except for the stretched first syllable of 'weekend'. However, this lends the melody a more musically satisfying, syncopated feel and is close *enough* to speech to be understood by the target audience already familiar with the vocabulary. At a micro-level, therefore, we engaged with Dilemma 1 (see Section 4.6.2) and reconciled the potentially competing priorities of musicality and speech proximity.

The brief also highlighted the popularity of martial arts in the target context, which reminded us to ensure that the song was culturally aware and relevant to the lives of its target audience (De Vries, 2010; see Section 4.6.1, Criteria 2, 3, and 4). However, there were no obvious opportunities for rhyme within the limited vocabulary provided, raising the issue of whether additional vocabulary was required (see Section 4.6.2, Dilemma 3). However, by using 'Saturday', 'Sunday', and 'day', we were able to create end rhymes. The draft lyrics were as follows

WHAT DO YOU DO AT THE WEEKEND?

Chorus
What do you do at the weekend?
What do you do all day?
What do you do at the weekend,
On Saturday and Sunday?

Verse
I play football and tennis,
And I do karate.
I chat to my friends
And maybe go to a party.
But I don't visit grandma
And I don't visit grandpa
Because they both live far away.

Verse
What do you do at the weekend?
What do you do all day?
What do you do at the weekend?
On Saturday and Sunday?

These were reviewed and subsequently signed off, though minor amendments were made to the first and last lines of the verse ('tennis' was replaced with 'make models', and 'both' was removed). The final lyrics and melody were as shown in Figure 2 and Audio 1.

> **Audio 1** 'What Do You Do at the Weekend?'. Audio file available at www.cambridge.org/Parkinson
> **Source**: *Open Up*. Reproduced by permission of Oxford University Press.

Figure 2 'What Do You Do at the Weekend?'

As this example illustrates, then, the songwriting process is initiated by a technical brief through which the lead author and the publisher communicate extra-musical, pedagogic, and linguistic requirements which impose thematic, lexical, and other constraints on the songwriting choices. Our first deliverable output was a draft of the lyrics, which contained no explicit musical information. However, from the very outset our creative decision-making was driven by musical concerns, and the identification of a melodically satisfying hook preceded the lyric writing, as is almost always the case. A number of evaluative considerations and dilemmas arose even at this early stage (see Section 4.6.2, Criteria 2, 3, and 4 and Dilemmas 1 and 3).

5.2 'Where Were You Last Night?': Emotional Engagement Through Deixis and Danceability

It can be challenging to write emotionally engaging lyrics from the very limited pools of the target language associated with coursebook units (see Section 4.6.2, Dilemma 3). The directness of the target language in the early stages of learning (e.g., 'I like pizza') also stands in contrast to the oblique, often metaphorical constructions that are central to the narrative functioning and appeal of pop music. Luckily, learners acquire some deictic words (e.g., 'you', 'me', 'this', 'that', 'then', 'now') at early stages of English language learning. As discussed in Section 3.1.2, deictic vocabulary is often used to write evocative choruses that, whether or not they correspond to specific details in verses, have an oblique quality that invites listeners to situate themselves at the song's centre and project their own real or imagined experiences onto it. For example, the chorus to Jennifer Lopez's 'Waiting for Tonight' establishes a non-specific spatio-temporal and interpersonal context through temporal ('tonight', 'here'), spatial ('here'), and person ('you', 'my') deictic vocabulary. This lends the song a timeless and universal resonance, bringing to each listener's mind their own 'tonight', 'here', and 'you'. In our experience, deictic choruses such as this pair well with melodramatic melodies and chord sequences that might sound absurd set against more direct or conspicuously childish lyrics (e.g., 'Let's tidy up our room'). In an ELT song context, deictic lyrics also sound closer to 'real' pop songs, and we regularly use deictic vocabulary in choruses to heighten songs' emotional resonance where the target vocabulary is particularly prosaic.

In 2020, we were commissioned to write the songs for a six-level English course for Spanish primary school learners aged six to twelve. In addition to songs that would appeal to young children, we therefore also needed to write songs that would appeal to children in early adolescence. As discussed in Section 3.2.1, this is a stage when children's musical tastes narrow, are woven into their emerging sense of identity and group belonging, and reflect their heightened emotionality (see Dilemma 8).

The six-level course was pitched at Beginner to Elementary levels (Common European Framework of Reference (CEFR) PRE-A1–A1+). For the levels aimed at older children, the challenge was therefore to write songs that sounded 'real' and resonated with learners' lives and listening habits beyond the school context (De Vries, 2010), yet remained age-appropriate and stayed within the target language as far as possible (see Section 4.6.2, Dilemma 2). One brief was for a song about 'City Life'. As with the previous example, the purpose was to consolidate the target vocabulary acquired in the preceding coursebook unit; the song would form the basis of a 'gap-fill' activity. The song also engaged with the theme of leisure activities but centred on locations in an urban environment (e.g., 'restaurant', 'stadium'), rather than activities. The grammar focus was past simple constructions using the verb 'to be', and there was a requirement for question-and-answer constructions, including the question 'where were you last night?', and for positive and negative replies (e.g., 'I wasn't at the theatre', 'I was at home').

The brief also established some non-linguistic, pedagogically functional requirements (Vinge, 2017). Firstly, in line with the vision for the coursebook, the song and the accompanying activities needed to invite children's responses and reactions on an emotional level. Secondly, the song needed to be not too grown-up and to depict fun experiences. Thirdly, the protagonists needed not to appear too affluent.

Of the target language set out in the brief, the question 'where were you last night?' immediately stood out for having all three deictic dimensions (spatial, temporal, and personal) and was therefore an obvious choice for the song's vocal hook (see Section 4.6.2, Criterion 10). It also offered a structuring device for the rest of the lyrics (question-and-answer). Accordingly, we used it as the basis for the song's main vocal hook, around which the other vocabulary is presented in answers and follow-up questions (see Figure 3 and Audio 2).

> **Audio 2** 'Bowling Alley' A section. Audio file available at www.cambridge.org/Parkinson
> **Source**: *Open Up*. Reproduced by permission of Oxford University Press.

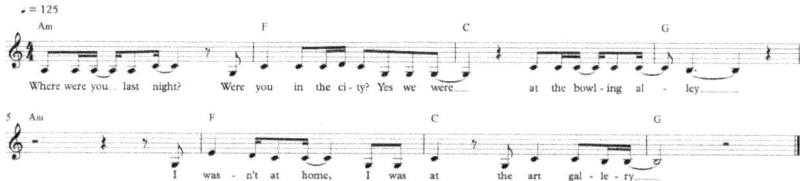

Figure 3 'Bowling Alley' A section

We set these lyrics against an Am-F-C-G chord progression, a common progression in pop music[15] that, to us at least, has both a sombre and a redemptive quality, owing to the movement between the minor 'home' chord (Am) and its relative major chord (C). This supported a strong melody but, to our ears, also lent an anguished, longing, or even accusatory connotation to the line 'where were you last night?' when sung in isolation (perhaps the singer is doubting the fidelity of their romantic partner?). This highlights how, as Askerøi (2017) observed, a song's music attenuates the meaning of the lyrics. Here, the music imbues the lyrics with an adult connotation[16] which – notwithstanding the specific vocabulary and context cues elsewhere in the lyrics – might *feel* age-inappropriate to some listeners. Given that concerns around age-appropriateness were raised in the brief, we were particularly conscious of ensuring that the song didn't sound too grown-up.

At the same time, however, the brief reminded us that songs needed to be engaging emotionally, in line with the coursebook's holistic aim of 'develop[ing] [children's] emotional wellbeing and help[ing] them make sense of their world' (Palin et al., 2023). To offset the potentially negative emotional valence of the Am-F-C-G chord progression, we added a B section composed of the same chords (F-C-Am-G) but establishing the relative major (C) chord as the 'home'. In addition, we gave the song an upbeat tempo and a danceable, 'four-to-the-floor' house beat (Criterion 7), both attributes thought to induce positive emotions in young listeners (Bhat et al., 2014; Janata et al., 2012; Maloy, 2018; see also Section 3.4.1).

Although the A and B sections address the language requirements set out in the brief, we felt that the song sounded incomplete and needed another transition. We decided therefore to include a C section based on the same chords as the A section but with a marimba motif in place of a vocal (Audio 3).

> **Audio 3** 'Bowling Alley' C section. Audio file available at www.cambridge.org/Parkinson
> **Source**: *Open Up*. Reproduced by permission of Oxford University Press.

As well as reinforcing the song's danceability, this riff serves two purposes. Firstly, it constitutes another hook (see Section 4.6.2, Criterion 10) and thus an additional opportunity to embed the song in the listener's memory. Secondly, it establishes space between the song's lyrical passages, providing respite from the active listening required by the proposed gap-fill exercise detailed in the brief.

---

[15] Well-known examples (or of vi–IV–I–V in other keys) include Lady Gaga's 'Poker Face', Joan Osborne's 'One of Us', John Legend's 'All of Me', and Adele's 'Hello'.
[16] Alternatively, the imagined scenario evoked by the deictic lyrics lend the chords a negative valence! – see Section 2.2.

In this example, then, we can see how the song's emotional impact – and by extension its potential to engage learners (see Section 2.4) – is determined by a number of interacting linguistic and musical factors. Paying attention to this interaction helped us to better align the song with the brief and ensure that the pedagogically functional, as well as pedagogically intentional, aims were met (Vinge, 2017).

5.3 'Pencil Case': Reconciling Linguistic, Pedagogical, and Musical Priorities

Another brief from the same coursebook series called for a song for beginner learners on the theme of 'my things'. The purpose of the song was to consolidate the target vocabulary, which included personal items associated with school (e.g., 'bag', 'book', 'pencil'), the question sentence 'where's my ____?', and the answer sentence 'it's on/in/under the ____'.

As with the previous examples, the question-and-answer vocabulary offered a potential structuring device for the lyrics. However, there were few opportunities for rhyme and limited options for where the objects might be located. We noticed, though, that two objects in the list, the pencil case and the bag, are receptacles. The vocabulary could therefore be collated into two verses – a pencil case verse and a bag verse – featuring extensive repetition within and across verses of the target question-and-answer language (Criterion 9):

Verse 1
Where is my pen? It's in my pencil case.
Where is my rubber? It's in my pencil case.
Where is the pencil? It's in my pencil case.

Verse 2
Where is my tablet? It's in my bag.
Where is my book? It's in my bag.
Where is the water bottle? It's in my bag.

Of course, if, as is common in pop music, each line were to be set across two bars, the verses would be an unusual six bars long. Sections of four, eight, and sixteen bars are the norm across most genres of popular music, and enculturated listeners would therefore expect an eight-bar verse (see Section 4.6.2, Criterion 8). Our solution was a final line for each verse, which served as a 'punchline':

But where is my pencil case?!
But where is my bag?!

Figure 4 'Pencil Case' demo

As a 'moment of salient appeal' (Smith, 2009, p. 311), this punchline became the song's hook (Criterion 10) and, happily, did not require any non-target vocabulary (see Section 4.6.2, Dilemma 2).

In most of our songs, the lyrics for a verse or chorus begin on the first beat of a bar. Writing lyrics in this way makes it easy for listeners to anticipate the start of the vocal, which can be signalled within the song by features such as cadences, drum-fills, or count-ins. However, it is common in popular music for vocal melodies, and particularly choruses, to begin with an anacrusis in the previous 'pick-up' bar (see discussion of twelve-bar blues, Section 2.2), with the lyrical phrase beginning before the stressed beat of the first bar proper and a strong syllable landing on the first beat of the first bar proper.[17] In some instances, the most intuitive and pop-sounding melodies that arise during an ELT songwriting session feature anacruses. As we began to experiment with melodies for 'Pencil Case' around a country shuffle rhythm, we landed on a satisfying stepwise melody that began with an anacrusis and placed each personal item (the target vocabulary) on the first beat of the bar (see Figure 4, Audio 4):

> **Audio 4** 'Pencil Case' demo. Audio file available at www.cambridge.org/Parkinson
> **Source**: *Open Up*. Reproduced by permission of Oxford University Press.

Here, then, we encountered a dilemma of whether to prioritise musicality over the pedagogically and prosodically optimal placement of lyrics within regular metric parameters to make them easier to anticipate. We negotiated this dilemma by evaluating the melody in relation to accessibility (see Section 4.6.1, Criterion 6), speech proximity (Section 4.6.2, Dilemma 1), and pedagogical purpose (Section 4.6.1, Criterion 5). Despite the anacrusis, the melody is uncomplicated and displays many archetypal traits of children's music. Indeed, though we were unaware of Maloy's (2018) children's music quotient at the time, the song possesses

---

[17] Examples include the choruses of 'Wrecking Ball' by Miley Cyrus and 'Firework' by Katy Perry.

almost all of its musical and lyrical criteria: 'scale-wise melodies'; 'melodic intervals of up to a sixth'; 'a reliance on tonic, subdominant and dominant chords' (here A, D, and E, though we also incorporated B minor seventh and C sharp minor seventh chords to add emotional depth – see Section 3.4.3); 'use of a major key'; 'regular common time signatures'; 'obvious and regular rhythms'; 'high levels of metric repetition'; and 'short, discrete lyrical phrases' (p. 34). We therefore decided that the melody was age-appropriate (see Section 4.6.1, Criterion 3) and accessible to listeners without musical training (Section 4.6.1, Criterion 6). In terms of speech proximity (Section 4.6.2, Dilemma 1), we observed that no syllables are truncated or stretched (except the melismatic 'where' in bars eight and nine), and the metre is broadly consonant with natural speech. In terms of specific pedagogical purpose (Section 4.6.1, Criterion 5), the melody amply facilitates the consolidation of the target vocabulary through its repetitiveness (Section 4.6.1, Criterion 9) and sing-ability (Section 4.6.1, Criterion 6). Beyond specific applications, the musicality of the melody enhances the song's aesthetic appeal and, thereby, its potential to engage learners and stimulate a positive learning environment.

The positive feedback on our demo confirmed our conviction that the song's melody is intuitive and catchy. However, we were surprised to discover that, in its current form, the song did not fulfil its designated pedagogical intentions. Owing to our having instinctively privileged melodic shape over linguistic precision, we had absent-mindedly deviated from the brief by splitting the contraction *where's* into its constituent words ('where is') so as to pair each monosyllabic word with a half beat ('where is my pen?'). Accordingly, we had to revisit the melody to accurately accommodate the target vocabulary. This was straightforward to do, but slightly undermined the satisfying, scale-wise-descending figure at the end of the verse. This was a minor change, however, and strict adherence to the target language was prioritised over the (marginally) optimal melodic shape. The final verse melody is as transcribed in Figure 5 (Audio 5).

Audio 5 Revised melody for 'Pencil Case'. Audio file available at www.cambridge.org/Parkinson
Source: *Open Up*. Reproduced by permission of Oxford University Press.

Figure 5 Revised melody for 'Pencil Case'

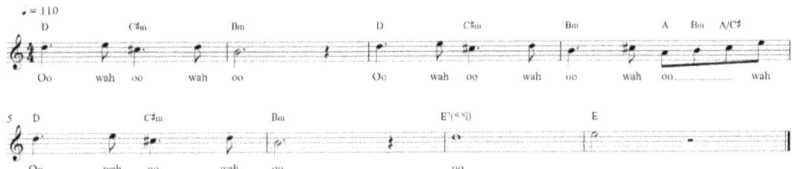

Figure 6 Non-verbal section of 'Pencil Case'

Although the two verses cover all the target language, we felt that the song was musically incomplete. As with 'Bowling Alley', we opted for an instrumental interlude based around a re-sequencing of the same chords used in the verse. As discussed in relation to 'Bowling Alley', instrumental passages provide respite from active listening, as well as an instrumental hook (see Section 4.6.1, Criterion 10). While we were satisfied with the chord structure, we felt that the harmonica melody was not hooky enough. After further experimentation, we found that it was stronger when sung using non-lexical 'oohs' and 'aahs' (see Figure 6). In our experience clients can be resistant to non-lexical vocables in ELT songs (see Section 2.5), believing them to be superfluous to, or even distracting from, the target language. We were therefore concerned that the author or the publisher might dislike this section. However, by double-tracking and harmonising the vocal and saturating some tracks in reverb, we achieved a choral feel that – to our ears – was less distracting and instead added texture to the instrumental, as well as enhancing the song's contemporary indie-pop feel (Audio 6). The clients happily agreed and the arrangement was taken forward.

> **Audio 6** Non-verbal section of 'Pencil Case'. Audio file available at www.cambridge.org/Parkinson
> **Source**: *Open Up*. Reproduced by permission of Oxford University Press.

5.4 Speech Proximity, Accent, and Pace

In the examples discussed so far, the balancing of musical, lyrical, and pedagogical considerations predominantly occurred in the initial songwriting and pre-production stages, rather than during the final recording session. Yet, even in the best-planned projects, unforeseen issues, particularly around pronunciation, pace, accent, and stress emphasis, can arise during the final recording when focus is firmly on the singer's delivery.

In the opening line of 'Bowling Alley', the three syllables of 'the city' are spaced a sixteenth note apart (see Figure 2). The truncated rhythm of this figure led the singer to pronounce the consonant *t* as *d* (/ˈsɪt̬.i/) as per North American Englishes (see Section 4.6.2, Dilemma 3). Nobody had noticed this

Figure 7 'Bowling Alley' revised melody

during the writing or pre-production stages, and it was highlighted during the recording session by the singer, a native Canadian but long-time UK resident. To mitigate the risk of the author or the publisher later rejecting the recording, we recorded an alternative take with the *t* enunciated, but this sounded forced and unnatural. Following a discussion and exchange of ideas among the songwriters, the session singer, and the publisher representative, we agreed to record a variation of the melody with the syllables stretched out to support a more natural delivery (see Figure 7 and Audio 7).

> **Audio 7** 'Bowling Alley' revised melody. Audio file available at www.cambridge.org/Parkinson
> **Source**: *Open Up*. Reproduced by permission of Oxford University Press.

Ultimately it was decided that variations in pronunciation were fine; after all, there were other, albeit less conspicuous, instances of 'American' pronunciation throughout the song (such as 'last' as /læst/), the singer's accents were indeterminate, and nowhere was the comprehensibility of the target language jeopardised by pronunciation. In the end, both versions were included in the final recording (the original in the intro chorus and the alternative version in the other choruses). Nonetheless, this example illustrates how anxieties around pronunciation, particularly in relation to the British/American English distinction, can arise in the studio and require on-the-spot musical decisions.

Sometimes issues can relate to the pace of articulation, rather than accent. Another song, 'What's in the Classroom?', has lyrics as follows:

> What's in the classroom? Let's look inside.
> Open the door, open your eyes.
> I can see a blue poster, a red chair, and a whiteboard.
> I can see three brown desks, a cupboard, and a green bin.

During the vocal recording, the publisher representative flagged that the delivery of the words 'I can see a' was perhaps too fast for young learners to sing along to. These were originally set to sixteenth notes (see Figure 8 and

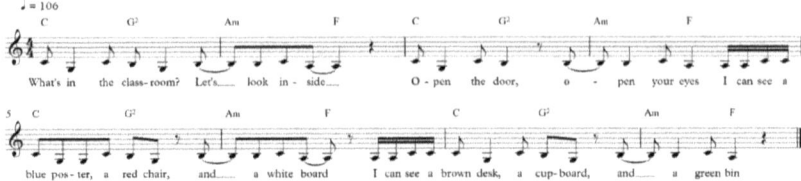

Figure 8 'What's in the Classroom?' original demo

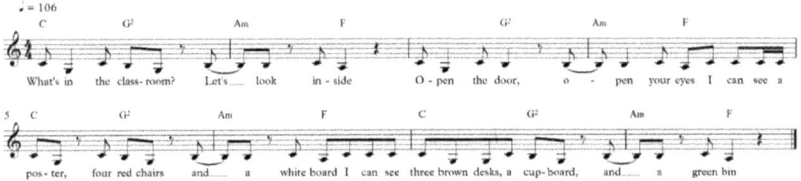

Figure 9 'What's in the Classroom?' revised melody

Audio 8). As with 'Bowling Alley', we auditioned some alternatives, ultimately recording a version that retained the sixteenth notes for 'see a' but set 'I' and 'can' to eighth notes. The word 'blue' was also removed to create more space (see Figure 9 and Audio 9).

Audio 8 'What's in the Classroom?' original demo. Audio file available at www.cambridge.org/Parkinson

Source: *Open Up*. Reproduced by permission of Oxford University Press.

Audio 9 'What's in the Classroom?' revised melody. Audio file available at www.cambridge.org/Parkinson

Source: *Open Up*. Reproduced by permission of Oxford University Press.

However, in this revised version there is no rest between the end of the second and the start of the third lines; both versions therefore had inherent 'problems'. It is common in ELT songwriting to have to make this kind of 'micro-decision' between two or more imperfect options, and, as with other examples, the final decision was made discursively through the weighing of the relative merits and hazards against different priorities.

5.5 Lyrical, Musical, and Sonic Alignment

As we discussed in Section 2, songs communicate meaning across their lyrical and musical aspects. While lyrical (i.e., linguistic) meaning is paramount in an ELT context, the role of music in fostering cohesive learning environments and engaging learners should not be neglected. Earlier examples in this section have illustrated how musical concerns are negotiated and reconciled with linguistic objectives, particularly in relation to vocal melody. As discussed in Section 2.3, however, pop songs' sonic environments – comprising their instrumental arrangements and the creative manipulation of sound sources through recording technologies – mediate the meanings conveyed by the lyrics and voice. In particular, meaning is imparted by sonic markers (Askerøi, 2017) – expressive devices marked by particular spatio-temporal associations. We make use of sonic markers in our ELT songwriting, albeit to varying degrees and in different ways depending on the brief, in order to ensure that there is emotional and sometimes thematic consonance across the music and lyrics (see Section 4.6.1, Criterion 11). This can range from markers associated with times and spaces that are explicit or implicit in the target language (such as sleigh bells in a Christmas song), to those associated with a musical genre, scene, or tradition.

Carnival and festival songs, with target language covering items and activities associated with public celebrations, are a common request. In writing the music to accompany such language, we seek to evoke the festive atmosphere of a carnival through sonic markers that connote musical genres associated with well-known carnival locations such as Brazil, New Orleans, and Notting Hill in London, as well as sounds associated with such settings. In one example, 'Carnival in Town Last Night', we overlaid a reggaeton-inspired beat performed on a cajon and electronic drums, a syncopated piano riff (using an 'Afro-Cuban Piano' sample instrument), maracas, and timbales. We also incorporated a brass melody as an instrumental hook, which recurred after each (deictic) chorus (Audio 10).

Audio 10 'Carnival in Town Last Night'. Audio file available at www.cambridge.org/Parkinson

Source: *Open Up*. Reproduced by permission of Oxford University Press.

In contrast, for another song, 'Carnival Time', we opted for a Zydeco-inspired accordion and woodwind-led arrangement (Audio 11). Our aim with such arrangements is not stylistic accuracy according to a particular musical tradition, or even approximation or pastiche. Rather, combining carnivalesque sonic markers – which, notwithstanding their particular provenance, are now well-established within mainstream global pop – helps to conjure an inclusive, festive atmosphere that will hopefully resonate with learners whether or not they have experience of, or cultural links to, a particular tradition or location

---

Audio 11 'Carnival Time'. Audio file available at www.cambridge.org/Parkinson

Source: *Open Up*. Reproduced by permission of Oxford University Press.

(see Section 4.6.1, Criterion 6; see also our earlier discussion of collective cultural memory regardless of personal experience, in Section 2.3).

5.6 'What Is a Family?': Cultural Representation and Implicit Ideology

Ideological values and assumptions inhere in the themes, settings, and characters found in ELT curricula and usually reflect the social mores of the producing and/or target market contexts (Mishan, 2022). We have found that anxieties about diversity, inclusivity, and cultural sensitivity (see Section 4.6.2, Dilemma 5) can emerge even around seemingly innocuous and universal themes.

We have received several briefs for songs on the theme of family, for which the target vocabulary is usually mum (or mom), dad, brother, sister, grandma, grandpa, uncle, aunty, and cousin, usually listed in that order. However, the heteronormative, two-parent family implied by this target vocabulary is not representative of the increasingly diverse range of family structures found globally and may not correspond to young learners' own family make-ups. In the interests of inclusive representation, therefore, we have often been asked to depict family units with step-parents and step-siblings. However, while blended families are rarely controversial, depictions of LGBTQI+ inclusive families can cause trepidation among some publishers and authors and might even be explicitly proscribed in socially conservative target markets (though we have not ourselves encountered this).

Of course, some clients do actively commission songs featuring non-heteronormative families. One example is a family song we wrote and produced for the British Council, 'What Is a Family?', which engages directly with the theme of diverse family units.[18] The chorus, with which the song opens, challenges the notion of a 'normal' or 'typical' family by asking:

> What is a family?
> It means different things to different people.
> What is a family?
> It means different things to you and me.

The verses then introduce different family configurations and experiences:

> You can have one mum,
> You can have one dad,
> You can have two mums,
> You can have two dads.
>
> . . .
>
> You can have a stepmum,
> You can have a stepdad,

---

[18] Creative Listening (2020d).

> Be raised by your grandma
> Or by your grandad.
> ...

It is conceivable, however, that these lyrics, and the accompanying animated video (see Figure 10), might be interpreted by teachers in some markets as inappropriate and even – given the British Council's cultural influence agenda – as a form of cultural imperialism, since they depict a Western liberal social and moral paradigm that is far from universal (see Section 3.3). This highlights that ELT songwriting, as a form of cultural production, is *inevitably* ideological, and that, in the globalised domain of ELT, ideological tensions can arise even around depictions of the everyday (see Figure 10).

5.7 Summary

In this section we have explored the creative decision-making processes undergirding our ELT songwriting practice through specific examples. In Section 6, we look more closely at the nature and dynamics of collaboration between multidisciplinary experts in the creation of ELT songs.

6 Multidisciplinary Collaboration in ELT Songwriting: Specialist, Adaptive, and Relational Expertise

As professional songwriters, we are commissioned to write ELT songs based on our specialist expertise in music composition, lyric writing, and production. As contracted service providers, we are responsible for undertaking the specified work and producing the required outputs to meet the client's expectations. However, as highlighted across Sections 4 and 5, the creative decision-making behind ELT songwriting is contingent upon extra-musical factors that sit within other stakeholders' areas of expertise. Successful ELT songwriting therefore requires active input from, and *collaboration among*, multidisciplinary experts, all of whom advocate for different priorities (see Section 4). In this regard, ELT songwriting differs from other forms of collaborative songwriting that are better represented in the research literature, where the collaboration under focus is usually that between co-songwriters, and where the evaluative criteria are mainly aesthetic and correspond to the songwriters' tastes and preferences (i.e., what 'feels' right; see Section 4.4). In this final section we focus more closely on the multidisciplinary collaborations underpinning the practice of ELT songwriting.

Figure 10 Stills from the animated video for 'What Is a Family?'

6.1 Sites and Modes of Collaboration

The process of songwriting proper (setting words to music, composing melodies and harmonic structures, and so on) is undertaken solely by the songwriting team. However, collaboration with other experts occurs in different ways, in different environments, and at different stages, in the creation of ELT songs.

6.1.1 Discursive Planning

As we discussed in Section 5.1, projects are usually initiated with a meeting between experts including (but not limited to) the course author(s), the publisher representative, and the songwriting team. This meeting sets out the parameters, expectations, and timelines, and builds rapport. After this initial meeting, interactions take place via online documents and technologies (such as Slack, Zoom, GoogleDocs, Dropbox, and of course email). As discussed in Section 5.1, the subsequent written brief also has a communicative and a collaborative function, setting out requirements and inviting responses. As we discuss in Section 6.2, discursive engagement is crucial for establishing the common knowledge, shared goals, and mutual recognition necessary for successful collaboration among multidisciplinary experts.

6.1.2 Dialogic Feedback

Once a brief has been agreed, one of the first deliverables is a demo. This can be anything from a simple recording of acoustic guitar and vocals to a relatively full arrangement, depending on the nature of the song, the time frame, and our relationship with the client.

Inviting stakeholders to participate in musical decision-making at demo stage helps to ensure that everyone feels invested and can ward against dissatisfaction later when changes can be costly or even impossible. In our experience, however, clients' ability to envisage an end-product from a demo can vary depending on their prior experience of working on musical projects and their level of musical training. Furthermore, as discussed in Sections 4.1 and 4.3, musically untrained listeners can lack the vocabulary to verbally articulate their responses or expectations. We find that inexperienced listeners can often use vague terms to describe how a song feels, particularly in negative assessments (e.g., 'can it be less edgy?', 'this song is a bit moody'). Clarifying what clients mean is vital to ensuring that their expectations are met, and where possible we discuss feedback with clients via live exchange environments such as Zoom calls, as opposed to email. This allows us to seek clarification, assist clients and collaborators in isolating and describing issues, and suggest alternative approaches. As we discuss in Section 6.2, there is a pedagogical dimension to these interactions in that we support clients and collaborators to develop descriptive capacity and to better understand the distance between a demo and a final recording in terms of refinement and production values. Reciprocally, a dialogic approach to feedback enables others to identify misunderstandings or knowledge gaps on our part around requirements of curricula, matters of linguistic precision, and/or alignment with wider coursebook objectives.

6.1.3 In the Recording Studio

Usually, ELT recording sessions are attended by a publisher representative (typically a member of the editorial team), the songwriting/production team, and the session singers (child singers are each accompanied by a parent or guardian). Depending on budget, an in-house engineer and a studio assistant may also be present. For large projects, there can be upwards of ten people present in the studio at the same time. This can be distracting or overwhelming for those with little experience of recording environments. Studio spaces are also emotionally intense environments 'privileged to the most intimate moments of musical creativity and emotive performances' (Watson and Ward, 2013, p. 2907). These factors exert significant pressure on a studio session, which can jeopardise productivity and quality. Management of space, and the interactions therein, is therefore essential to a successful recording session.

Those present at an ELT song recording session have diverse backgrounds, needs, and expectations that we need to attend to sensitively. Children need regular encouragement, fun activities to keep them occupied, and friendly interactions. Parents often have questions about the project and like to take photos or videos of their children singing. Client representatives are often anxious about time and unsettled by unexpected delays, such as if we have to reboot the studio computer or stop to edit recordings. Part of our role in these settings is to induct musically inexperienced collaborators into the cultures and workflows of the studio environment in order to achieve a positive atmosphere that elicits quality performances from the musicians, commonly known as 'vibe'. Watson and Ward (2013) theorise vibe in terms of 'emotional labour performances' (p. 2904) on the part of producers and engineers, who must 'induce or suppress [their own] feeling in order to sustain the outward countenance that produces the proper state of mind in others' (Hochschild, 1983, p. 7, cited in Watson and Ward, 2013, p. 2905). Given the professional diversity of an ELT songwriting session, we need to establish an inclusive vibe that enables everyone present to undertake their role effectively.

6.1.4 Collaborative Listening

Because vocal precision and clarity are paramount in ELT songs, we monitor singers' delivery fastidiously. Where in a non-ELT context a producer might seek to capture a singer's idiosyncrasies in pursuit of an authentic and characterful vocal, here we need to ensure that consonants and vowels are sounded accurately, and 'iron out' stylistic embellishments such as rasp, breathiness, fall-offs, and melisma. This raises Dilemma 1 (Section 4.6.2), however. Singers use these techniques – often instinctively – to impart character and emotion; removing them can be detrimental to a song's musicality and limit its appeal and potential to engage learners. While publisher representatives tend to prioritise speech proximity, as producer-songwriters we instinctively incline towards musically successful performances. While the publisher's decision is ultimately respected, having advocates for these competing priorities in the studio space helps us to reconcile them more successfully.

As with feedback on demo recordings, different collaborators notice different issues during studio listening and need to be able to isolate and explain issues to others in accessible ways. For example, if a publisher representative observes that a singer's pronunciation of a word or phrase goes against the project's linguistic requirements, they need to be able to convey this issue to the songwriter-producer, who must in turn communicate the issue to the (usually linguistically untrained) singer. In such situations, we would typically mediate a live interaction over the talkback system between the singer in the booth and the publisher representative in the control room. This might involve encouraging the publisher representative (who may not be confident singing) to model the ideal delivery, or modelling the delivery ourselves and inviting the publisher representative to critique it until we get it right. Through such trial-and-error interactions, a relational dynamic is established that, over time, fosters common knowledge.

6.2 ELT Songwriting: A Collaborative Model

Figure 11 is an attempt to represent the nature of collaboration on ELT songwriting projects. The overlapping circles depict the three main domains of specialist expertise within the multidisciplinary domain of ELT songwriting. Each domain is represented by an expert practitioner. As songwriters, our principal domain of specialist expertise is *musical*, encompassing knowledge of 'material' aspects such as 'words, melodies, instrumentation, sound effects and [other] sonic parameters' and 'immaterials' such as normative conventions around song structure, length, and so on (Whiting, 2023, p. 144). Because we also act as producers and audio engineers on most projects, this domain also

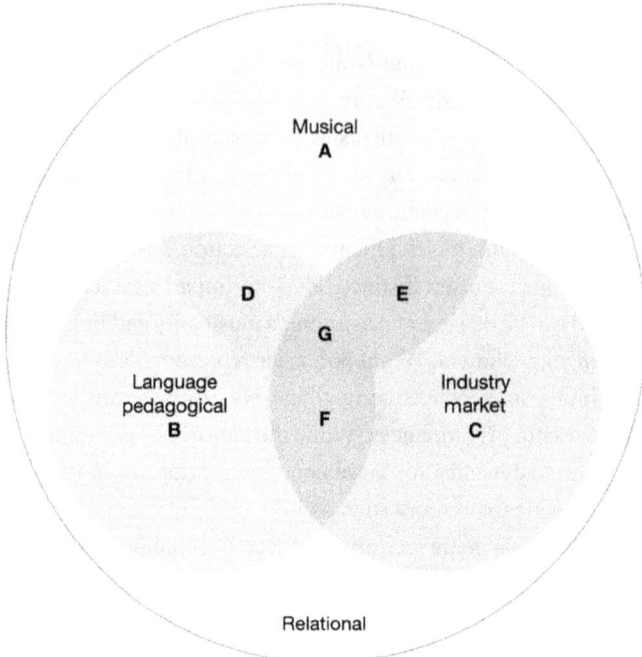

Figure 11 Multidisciplinary collaboration on ELT songs

comprises technical expertise relating to record production, studio management, mixing, mastering, and instrumental performance. Subcontracted session singers and studio engineers also sit within this domain of expertise. While individuals' profiles differ, all musical experts share an experiential knowledge of the workflows, spaces, and cultures that characterise the field of music creation.

As discussed in Section 4.2, ELT authors are usually former language teachers. Atkinson's (2021a) research revealed how ELT authors 'tap [into] knowledge and skills gained in the associated domains of English language and teacher training when writing ELT textbooks' (p. 604). Our model collates these domains together within the *language pedagogical* expertise domain. Publisher representatives hold extensive industry expertise, encompassing publishing-related practices, technologies and regulations, trends, target markets, and competitors' materials, and thus represent the *industry* expertise domain.

Within an ELT songwriting project, experts from each domain retain authority over, and work independently on, some 'pure' aspects of their work. For songwriters this includes instrumental performance, operating recording software and hardware, and so on; for a publisher representative this might include market research and copyright clearances; and for authors this might include matters of language and pedagogical techniques. These pure areas are represented in the model as A, B, and C.

As the overlapping portions of the model suggest, however, ELT songwriting, like any multidisciplinary undertaking, necessarily involves interaction across domains of expertise. Atkinson (2021a) proposed that experts in adjacent domains often apply cognate expertise from their own domain to solve problems in the adjacent domain, wherein they encounter challenge, adapt, and acquire new expertise. This represents an adaptive form of 'domain acquisition' as proposed by Thompson and Harding (2019), whereby newcomers learn 'a cultural tradition's language, symbol system, rules, skills, and techniques' (p. 160). Crucially, it also entails the development of 'adaptive expertise' (Atkinson, 2021a, p. 604), which belongs to neither specialist domain but relates to the *ability to* adapt. These areas of adjacent domain acquisition are represented as D, E, and F. In zone F, for example, ELT authors, though primarily *language pedagogical* experts, acquire additional and adaptive expertise in the adjacent domain of the ELT publishing industry, through 'squar[ing] pedagogical imperatives with publishing realities' (Atkinson, 2021b, p. 2). In zone E, songwriters extend their expertise into the *industry* domain through experiencing and adapting to the ELT industry's cultures, practices, and regulations. Publishers meanwhile adapt to and acquire expertise in the *musical* domain through activities such as listening to and feeding back on demo recordings, attending studio sessions, and so on. Authors and songwriters acquire additional and adaptive expertise in the *musical* and *language pedagogical* domains, respectively, through encountering and internalising different imperatives (musical, linguistic, pedagogical) surrounding the handling of language.

To summarise at this point, experts within the multidisciplinary domain of ELT songwriting possess specialist expertise in their home domain, acquire additional expertise in adjacent domains, and develop adaptive expertise. However, since multidisciplinary collaboration is a fundamentally social phenomenon, experts also need to develop what Edwards (2011) termed relational expertise. Edwards (2011) developed the notion of relational expertise through research on multidisciplinary teams working in child welfare settings, where experts with different knowledge and priorities, such as social workers, psychologists, teachers, and parents, work together to solve problems. Edwards' (2011) research revealed that, in such settings, 'the resources that others bring to collaborations on complex problems … can enhance understandings [and] enrich responses', but that 'working across practice boundaries … makes demands on practitioners' (p. 33). Accordingly, practitioners need an additional form of expertise that 'makes it possible to work with others to expand understandings of the work problem as … an "object of activity"' (Edwards, 2011,

p. 33). Relational expertise overlaps with adaptive expertise, but it concerns experts' interactions with others to generate common knowledge, rather than simply their acquisition of and adaptation to adjacent domains of expertise. It combines 'confident engagement with the knowledge that underpins one's own specialist practice, as well as a capacity to recognise and respond to what others might offer in local systems of distributed expertise' (Edwards, 2011, p. 33).

In our model, zones D, E, F, and G align with Edwards' (2011) description of socially constructed 'boundary spaces' with 'different communication systems, meaning systems, priorities, time-scales and so on', where 'the resources from different practices are brought together to expand interpretations of multifaceted tasks' (p. 35). Edwards (2011) explained that 'boundary talk' elicits differences, but also builds common knowledge that makes effective collaboration possible. Among the features of boundary work that foster common knowledge are 'clarifying the purpose of work and being open to alternatives'; 'understanding oneself and one's professional values better'; 'knowing how to know who'; 'taking a pedagogic stance at work'; 'being responsive to others: both professionals and clients'; 'rule-bending and risk-taking'; and 'learning from practice' (p. 35). Edwards (2011) also identified the importance of language and the need to make practice intelligible to others.

All of these features are pertinent to the practice of ELT songwriting and chime with our experiences of collaborating with experts from different domains. As explained in Section 6.1, active discussion is the primary means through which common knowledge is generated. As we discussed in Section 5, being open to alternatives beyond the orthodoxies of one's pure domain (such as, in our case, compromising on melodic shape to ensure that linguistic priorities are better met), sometimes bending the rules (such as a materials author conceding to the inclusion of non-target vocabulary in service to a more engaging hook), and knowing when to defer to the best-placed expert are all requisites of effective ELT songwriting. Boundary talk reveals differences in priorities and values, but also promotes recognition of what others bring, builds trust, and ultimately 'enhance[s] understanding' of and 'enriche[s] responses' to the object of activity, the ELT song (Edwards, 2011, p. 33).

Taking a 'pedagogic stance' in boundary spaces is also a crucial aspect of collaboration in ELT songwriting, particularly in relation to language and concepts. As we discussed in relation to dialogic feedback on demos and during studio sessions (Sections 6.1.1 and 6.1.2), collaborating experts need to take responsibility for building common knowledge by making their own knowledge accessible, coaching others to articulate their perspectives clearly, and checking to ensure that everyone has been understood correctly.

Each of the domains in our model also possesses categorical jargon that can be alienating and impede common knowledge. When operating within zone A, a songwriter and an engineer would communicate using technical language and acronyms (e.g., 'DAW' (digital audio workstation), 'comp', 'drop in', 'bounce'); however, such language is unsuitable for zones D and E, and concepts may need to be explained to authors and publisher representatives to build common knowledge. Instead, we describe concepts in plain language using generic terminology (e.g., 'software' instead of DAW, 'join together' instead of 'comp'), at least initially, until a sufficient degree of common knowledge has been achieved. In our experience, however, common knowledge, relational expertise, and adaptive expertise can be developed relatively quickly on large projects, providing, as Edwards (2011) advised, that time and resources are invested in building relationships and setting clear, shared goals.

6.3 Conclusion

In this Element we sought to address a surprising gap in the research literature by shedding light on the ELT song, a musical phenomenon engaged with by millions globally, through a focus on our own practice of ELT songwriting. Through literature review and reflective practice-led enquiry, we explored the multimodal nature of songs as musical and linguistic texts, the ways in which music and language interact in the context of a song to generate meaning, and the role that songs play in the education of young language learners. We considered the emergence and status of ELT songs as a form of pop music, a subgenre of children's music, a product of the multi-billion-dollar ELT industry, and a popular but little-understood classroom resource. Reflecting on our decade-long practice, we considered the expectations and priorities of different stakeholders involved in the creation, use, and reception of ELT songs, namely songwriters, coursebook authors, publishers, teachers, and young learners, and proposed a criteria and dilemma-based evaluative framework for ELT songs. We explored the decision-making behind ELT songwriting through examples from our practice, highlighting how dilemmas are encountered, negotiated, and resolved in collaboration with other stakeholders. Finally, we examined the nature of collaboration among multidisciplinary experts in the production of ELT songs and proposed a model for adaptive and relational expertise in ELT songwriting.

The insights contained in this Element have arisen primarily from our reflections on professional practice, undertaken both prior to and alongside engagement with the research literature. As such, this Element works to make tacit practice-based knowledge explicit and synthesises this practice knowledge with empirical insight and theory derived from academic research across usually discrete fields. In so doing, it enriches understanding of songwriting practice and songwriter metacognition, through a focus on an under-researched but widespread form of songwriting, as well as ELT materials writing and the metacognition of ELT professionals other than teachers.

While the artefacts of this practice – recorded songs, demos, song briefs, email exchanges, and recording projects – constituted a source of data and allowed for post hoc analysis, the study presented in this Element was not, strictly speaking, empirical. Nor was it practice-*based* or practice-*as*-research (Nelson, 2006) because we did not seek to address a pre-formulated research problematic through practice itself as the primary mode of inquiry. Furthermore, while this Element offers direct insight into *our* decision-making and experiences, and holds validity as an insider account, our interpretations of other stakeholders' positions and priorities are abductive and/or limited to our experience. Rigorous empirical studies are needed to address narrower research questions and elicit first-hand perspectives from other stakeholders within the field of ELT songs. We plan to undertake such studies going forward, particularly in relation to young learners' experiences with ELT songs. We hope also that readers may identify avenues for future research issuing from the insights presented in this Element.

References

Ajibade, Y., & Ndububa, K. (2008). Effects of word games, culturally relevant songs, and stories on students' motivation in a Nigerian English language class. *TESL (Teaching English as a Second Language) Canada Journal, 25*(2), 27–48. https://doi.org/10.18806/tesl.v26i1.128.

Akbari, R. (2008). Transforming lives: Introducing critical pedagogy into ELT classrooms. *ELT (English Language Teaching) Journal, 62*(3), 276–283. https://doi.org/10.1093/elt/ccn025.

Akbary, M., Shahriari, H., & Hosseini Fatemi, A. (2018). The value of song lyrics for teaching and learning English phrasal verbs: A corpus investigation of four music genres. *Innovation in Language Learning and Teaching, 12*(4), 344–356. https://doi.org/10.1080/17501229.2016.1216121.

Al Hosni, J. K. (2015). Globalization and the linguistic imperialism of the English language. *Arab World English Journal (AWEJ), 6*(1), 298–308. https://doi.org/10.24093/awej/vol6no1.23.

Almutairi, M., & Shukri, N. (2016). Using songs in teaching oral skills to young learners: Teachers' views and attitudes. *International Journal of Linguistics, 8*(6), 133–153. https://doi.org/10.5296/ijl.v8i6.10464.

Aniuranti, A. (2021). An investigation of song-based language teaching on tenses learning. *Economics, Social, and Humanities Journal (Esochum), 1*(1), 45–55.

Arthur, C. (2023). Why do songs get 'stuck in our heads'? Towards a theory for explaining earworms. *Music and Science, 6*. https://doi.org/10.1177/20592043231164581.

Askerøi, E. (2013). Reading pop production: Sonic markers and musical identity. Doctoral dissertation, University of Agder.

Askerøi, E. (2017). Pop music for kids: Sonic markers as narrative strategies in children's music. *Nordic Journal of Art and Research, 6*(2). https://doi.org/10.7577/information.v6i2.2277.

Atkinson, D. (2021a). The adaptive expertise of expert ELT textbook writers. *RELC (Regional Language Centre) Journal, 52*(3), 603–617. https://doi.org/10.1177/0033688219893119.

Atkinson, D. (2021b). Reconciling opposites to reach compromise during ELT textbook development. *Language Teaching Research, 28*(5), 1976–1996. https://doi.org/10.1177/13621688211040201.

Baker, S. (2001). 'Rock on, baby!': Pre-teen girls and popular music. *Continuum: Journal of Media and Cultural Studies, 15*(3), 359–371. https://doi.org/10.1080/10304310120086830.

Beaman, C. P. (2018). The literary and recent scientific history of the earworm: A review and theoretical framework. *Auditory Perception and Cognition*, *1*(1–2), 42–65. https://doi.org/10.1080/25742442.2018.1533735.

Beaman, C. P., & Williams, T. I. (2010). Earworms (stuck song syndrome): Towards a natural history of intrusive thoughts. *British Journal of Psychology*, *101*(4), 637–653. https://doi.org/10.1348/000712609x479636.

Becker, J. (1986). Is Western art music superior? *Musical Quarterly*, *72*(3), 341–359. https://doi.org/10.1093/mq/lxxii.3.341.

Bennett, J. (2012). Constraint, collaboration and creativity in popular songwriting teams. In D. Collins (ed.), *The Act of Musical Composition: Studies in the Creative Process* (pp. 139–170). Routledge.

Bentley, J. (2014). Report from TESOL 2014: 1.5 billion English learners worldwide. International TEFL Academy (ITA) blog. www.internationalteflacademy.com/blog/report-from-tesol-2-billion-english-learners-worldwide.

Bhat, A. S., Amith, V. S., Prasad, N. S., & Mohan, D. M. (2014). An efficient classification algorithm for music mood detection in Western and Hindi music using audio feature extraction. *Proceedings of the 2014 Fifth International Conference on Signal and Image Processing*, Bangalore, India, pp. 359–364. https://doi.org/10.1109/ICSIP.2014.63.

Bickford, T. (2007). Music of poetry and poetry of song: Expressivity and grammar in vocal performance. *Ethnomusicology*, *51*(3), 439–476. https://doi.org/10.2307/20174545.

Bickford, T. (2019). The kindie movement: Independent children's music in the United States since 2000. In S. Young & B. Ilari (eds.), *Music in Early Childhood: Multi-disciplinary Perspectives and Inter-disciplinary Exchanges* (vol. 27, pp. 223–233). Springer International. https://doi.org/10.1007/978-3-030-17791-1_14.

Bignell, J. (2017). Broadcasting children's music. *InFormation: Nordic Journal of Art and Research*, *6*(2). https://doi.org/10.7577/information.v6i2.2275.

Bokiev, D., & Ismail, L. (2021). Malaysian ESL teachers' beliefs and practices regarding the use of music and songs in second language teaching. *Qualitative Report*, *26*(5), 1497–1521. https://doi.org/10.46743/2160-3715/2021.4350.

Bonneville-Roussy, A., Rentfrow, P. J., Xu, M. K., & Potter, J. (2013). Music through the ages: Trends in musical engagement and preferences from adolescence through middle adulthood. *Journal of Personality and Social Psychology*, *105*(4), 703–717. https://doi.org/10.1037/a0033770.

Bonshor, M. (2023). Happy songs: These are the musical elements that make us feel good. *Conversation*, 30 March. http://theconversation.com/happy-songs-these-are-the-musical-elements-that-make-us-feel-good-201342.

Boothe, D., & West, J. (2015). English language learning through music and song lyrics – The performance of a lifetime. In *Conference Proceedings: The Future of Education* (pp. 248–252). Libreria universitaria. https://shorturl.at/re1kH.

Bouzid, H. A. (2016). Race and social class in Moroccan ELT textbooks. *EFL Journal, 1*(2), 113–127. https://doi.org/10.21462/eflj.v1i2.11.

Buckledee, S. J. (2010). Global English and ELT coursebooks. In C. Gagliardi & A. Maley (eds.), *EIL, ELF, Global English: Teaching and Learning Issues*, Linguistic Insights vol. 96 (pp. 141–151). Peter Lang.

Budairi, A. (2018). Traces of linguistic imperialism enacted through discursive strategies in ELT textbooks in Indonesia. *English Language Teaching Educational Journal, 1*(2), 49–64. https://doi.org/10.12928/eltej.v1i2.581.

Busse, V., Hennies, C., Kreutz, G., & Roden, I. (2021). Learning grammar through singing? An intervention with EFL primary school learners. *Learning and Instruction, 71*, 101372. https://doi.org/10.1016/j.learninstruc.2020.101372.

Cavarero, A. (2005). *For More Than One Voice: Toward a Philosophy of Vocal Expression*. Stanford University Press.

Chan, J. Y. H. (2019). The choice of English pronunciation goals: Different views, experiences and concerns of students, teachers and professionals. *Asian Englishes, 21*(3), 264–284. https://doi.org/10.1080/13488678.2018.1482436.

Chen, Y. C., & Chen, P. C. (2009). The effect of English popular songs on learning motivation and learning performance. *WHAMPOA: An Interdisciplinary Journal, 56*, 13–28. https://shorturl.at/Lkrdy.

Chesebro, J. W., Foulger, D. A., Naghman, J. E., & Yannelli, A. (1985). Popular music as a mode of communication, 1955–1982. *Critical Studies in Media Communication, 2*(2), 115–135. https://doi.org/10.1080/15295038509360071.

Chou, M. H. (2014). Assessing English vocabulary and enhancing young English as a foreign language (EFL) learners' motivation through games, songs, and stories. *Education 3–13, 42*(3), 284–297. https://doi.org/10.1080/03004279.2012.680899.

Codó, E., & McDaid, J. (2019). English language assistants in the 21st century: Nation-state soft power in the experience economy. *Language, Culture and Society, 1*(2), 219–243. https://doi.org/10.1075/lcs.00017.cod.

Cores-Bilbao, E., Fernández-Corbacho, A., Machancoses, F. H., & Fonseca-Mora, M. C. (2019). A music-mediated language learning experience: Students' awareness of their socio-emotional skills. *Frontiers in Psychology, 10*, 2238. https://doi.org/10.3389/fpsyg.2019.02238.

Coyle, Y., & Gómez Gracia, R. (2014). Using songs to enhance L2 vocabulary acquisition in preschool children. *ELT Journal, 68*(3), 276–285. https://doi.org/10.1093/elt/ccu015.

Creative Listening (2018). *The Magic Cat*. One Stop English. Macmillan. www.onestopenglish.com/download?ac=61600.

Creative Listening (2020a) 'Do Your Best'. In Robot Songs [animated song cycle]. Online video clip. www.youtube.com/watch?v=3wdEoldOGCc.

Creative Listening (2020b) 'Robot Says'. In Robot Songs [animated song cycle]. Online video clip. www.youtube.com/watch?v=VwJ59Dv7_Bs.

Creative Listening (2020c) 'Snack Time'. In Robot Songs [animated song cycle]. Online video clip. www.youtube.com/watch?v=3hRFGxWxggM.

Creative Listening (2020d) 'What Is a Family?' In Robot Songs [animated song cycle]. Online video clip. www.youtube.com/watch?v=tR3YC6XadKY.

Davis, G. M. (2017). Songs in the young learner classroom: A critical review of evidence. *ELT Journal*, 71(4), 445–455. https://doi.org/10.1093/elt/ccw097.

Deaville, J. (2011). *Music in Television: Channels of Listening*. Routledge.

Dell, F., & Elmedlaoui, M. (2008). *Poetic Meter and Musical Form in Tashlhiyt Berber Songs*. Berber Studies vol. 19. Rüdiger Köppe.

De Vries, P. (2010). What we want: The music preferences of upper primary school students and the ways they engage with music. *Australian Journal of Music Education*, 1, 3–16. www.learntechlib.org/p/54518/.

Dewaele, J.-M., Witney, J., Saito, K., & Dewaele, L. (2018). Foreign language enjoyment and anxiety: The effect of teacher and learner variables. *Language Teaching Research*, 22(6), 676–697. https://doi.org/10.1177/1362168817692161.

Dolean, D. D. (2016). The effects of teaching songs during foreign language classes on students' foreign language anxiety. *Language Teaching Research*, 20(5), 638–653. https://doi.org/10.1177/1362168815606151.

Dolean, D. D., & Dolean, I. (2014). The impact of teaching songs on foreign language classroom anxiety. *Philologica Jassyensia*, 10(1), 513–518.

Edwards, A. (2011). Building common knowledge at the boundaries between professional practices: Relational agency and relational expertise in systems of distributed expertise. *International Journal of Educational Research*, 50(1), 33–39. https://doi.org/10.1016/j.ijer.2011.04.007.

Engh, D. (2013). Why use music in English language learning? A survey of the literature. *English Language Teaching*, 6(2), 113–127. https://doi.org/10.5539/elt.v6n2p113.

European Commission / EACEA (European Education and Culture Executive Agency) / Eurydice (2023). *Key Data on Teaching Languages at School in Europe – 2023 Edition* [Eurydice Report]. Publications Office of the European Union. [Authored by P. Birch, N. Baïdak, I. de Coster, & D. Kocanova and alternatively referred to as the P. Birch Edition.] https://data.europa.eu/doi/10.2797/529032.

Faure-Carvallo, A., Gustems-Carnicer, J., & Guaus Termens, E. (2022). Music education in the digital age: Challenges associated with sound homogenization in music aimed at adolescents. *International Journal of Music Education*, *40*(4), 598–612. https://doi.org/10.1177/02557614221084315.

Feng, T. (2016). Development of morphological awareness through English songs: A case study. *Chinese Journal of Applied Linguistics*, *39*(2), 167–184. https://doi.org/10.1515/cjal-2016-0011.

Fernández de Cañete García, C., Pineda, I., & Waddell, G. (2022). Music as a medium of instruction (MMI): A new pedagogical approach to English language teaching for students with and without music training. *Language Teaching Research*. https://doi.org/10.1177/13621688221105769.

Frith, S. (1989). Why do songs have words? *Contemporary Music Review*, *5*(1), 77–96. https://doi.org/10.1080/07494468900640551.

Gagnon, L., & Peretz, I. (2003). Mode and tempo relative contributions to 'happy-sad' judgements in equitone melodies. *Cognition and Emotion*, *17*(1), 25–40. https://doi.org/10.1080/02699930302279.

Godding, N. (2021). Oxfordshire edtech targets £100M valuation in 2022 as it seeks global expansion after deal with TOKYO MX. *Business Magazine*, 6 October. https://shorturl.at/fbPRx.

Goldberg, A. E. (2003). Constructions: A new theoretical approach to language. *Trends in Cognitive Science*, *7*(5), 219–224. https://doi.org/10.1016/s1364-6613(03)00080-9.

Grant, R., & Wong, S. (2018). Addressing cultural bias in ELT materials. In J. I. Liontas (ed.), *The TESOL Encyclopedia of English Language Teaching* (pp. 1–8). John Wiley.

Green, L. (2017). *How Popular Musicians Learn: A Way Ahead for Music Education*. Routledge.

Guyer, A. E., Silk, J. S., & Nelson, E. E. (2016). The neurobiology of the emotional adolescent: From the inside out. *Neuroscience and Biobehavioral Reviews*, *70*, 74–85. https://doi.org/10.1016/j.neubiorev.2016.07.037.

Hamid, M. O. (2023). English as a Southern language. *Language in Society*, *52*(3), 409–432. https://doi.org/10.1017/S0047404522000069.

Hatfield, E., Cacioppo, J. T., & Rapson, R. L. (1994). *Emotional Contagion*. Cambridge University Press.

Herbert, R., & Dibben, N. (2018). Making sense of music: Meanings 10- to 18-year-olds attach to experimenter-selected musical materials. *Psychology of Music*, *46*(3), 375–391. https://doi.org/10.1177/0305735617713118.

Ho, W. C. (2017). Secondary school students' preferences for popular music and perceptions of popular music learned in school music education in

Mainland China. *Research Studies in Music Education*, *39*(1), 19–37. https://doi.org/10.1177/1321103x17700688.

Ho, W. C., & Law, W. W. (2009). Sociopolitical culture and school music education in Hong Kong. *British Journal of Music Education*, *26*(1), 71–84. https://doi.org/10.1017/s0265051708008292.

Hochschild, A. (1983). *The Managed Heart: Commercialisation of Human Feeling*. University of California Press.

Holden, J. (2013) *Influence and Attraction: Culture and the Race for Soft Power in the 21st Century*. British Council and Demos.

Huber, A. (2013). Mainstream as metaphor: Imagining dominant culture. In S. Baker, A. Bennett, & J. Taylor (eds.), *Redefining Mainstream Popular Music* (pp. 3–13). Routledge.

Hunter, P. G., & Schellenberg, E. G. (2010). Music and emotion. In M. Riess Jones, R. Fay, & A. Popper (eds.), *Music Perception*, Springer Handbook of Auditory Research vol. 36 (pp. 129–164). Springer.

Jakubowski, K., Finkel, S., Stewart, L., & Müllensiefen, D. (2017). Dissecting an earworm: Melodic features and song popularity predict involuntary musical imagery. *Psychology of Aesthetics, Creativity, and the Arts*, *11*(2), 122–135. https://doi.org/10.1037/aca0000090.

Janata, P., Tomic, S. T., & Haberman, J. M. (2012). Sensorimotor coupling in music and the psychology of the groove. *Journal of Experimental Psychology: General*, *141*(1), 54–75. https://doi.org/10.1037/a0024208.

Jordan, G., & Gray, H. (2019). We need to talk about coursebooks. *ELT Journal*, *73*(4), 438–446. https://doi.org/10.1093/elt/ccz038.

Juslin, P. N. (2013). From everyday emotions to aesthetic emotions: Towards a unified theory of musical emotions. *Physics of Life Reviews*, *10*(3), 235–266. https://doi.org/10.1016/j.plrev.2013.05.008.

Juslin, P. N., & Västfjäll, D. (2008). Emotional responses to music: The need to consider underlying mechanisms. *Behavioral and Brain Sciences*, *31*(5), 559–575. https://doi.org/10.1017/S0140525X08005293.

Kaminska, Z., & Woolf, J. (2000). Melodic line and emotion: Cooke's theory revisited. *Psychology of Music*, *28*(2), 133–153. https://doi.org/10.1177/0305735600282003.

Killingly, C., Lacherez, P., & Meuter, R. (2021). Singing in the brain: Investigating the cognitive basis of earworms. *Music Perception: An Interdisciplinary Journal*, *38*(5), 456–472. https://doi.org/10.1525/mp.2021.38.5.456.

Knudsen, E., & Markovic, D. (2021). United States of America: Country report. In H. K. Anheier and ifa (eds.), *The External Cultural Policy Monitor*. ifa (Institut für Auslandsbeziehungen). https://doi.org/10.17901/ecp.2021.034.

Kolchinsky, A., Dhande, N., Park, K., & Ahn, Y.-Y. (2017). The minor fall, the major lift: Inferring emotional valence of musical chords through lyrics. *Royal Society Open Science*, *4*(11), 170952. https://doi.org/10.1098/rsos.170952.

Krashen, S. (1982). *Principles and Practice in Second Language Acquisition*. Pergamon Press.

Krashen, S. D. (1983). The din in the head, input, and the language acquisition device. *Foreign Language Annals*, *16*(1), 41–44. https://doi.org/10.1111/j.1944-9720.1983.tb01422.x.

Kruse, A. J. (2016). Toward hip-hop pedagogies for music education. *International Journal of Music Education*, *34*(2), 247–260. https://doi.org/10.1177/0255761414550535.

Kumar, T., Akhter, S., Yunus, M. M., & Shamsy, A. (2022). Use of music and songs as pedagogical tools in teaching English as foreign language contexts. *Education Research International*, *2022*, 1–9. https://doi.org/10.1155/2022/3384067.

Kung, F. W. (2013). Rhythm and pronunciation of American English: Jazzing up EFL teaching through Jazz chants. *Asian EFL Journal*, *70*, 4–27. www.researchgate.net/publication/281853147.

Kuśnierek, A. (2016). The role of music and songs in teaching English vocabulary to students. *World Scientific News*, *43*(1), 1–55. https://typeset.io/pdf/the-role-of-music-and-songs-in-teaching-english-vocabulary-4igx1klbym.pdf.

Lamont, A., & Hargreaves, D. (2019). Musical preference and social identity in adolescence. In K. McFerran, P. Derrington, & S. Saarikallio (eds.), *Handbook of Music, Adolescents, and Wellbeing* (pp. 109–118). Oxford University Press.

LearnCube (2023). UK losing share in global ELT market. *LearnCube*. www.learncube.com/UK-ELT-market-losing-share.html.

Lee, J., & Schreibeis, M. (2021). Comprehensive review of the effect of using music in second language learning. In A. Burkette & T. Warhol (eds.), *Crossing Borders, Making Connections: Interdisciplinarity in Linguistics* (vol. 1, pp. 231–246). De Gruyter. https://doi.org/10.1515/9781501514371-016.

Legg, R. (2009). Using music to accelerate language learning: An experimental study. *Research in Education*, *82*(1), 1–12. https://doi.org/10.7227/rie.82.1.

Lieb, M. M. (2005). Popular music and its role in the EFL classroom. *KOTESOL Proceedings 2005 – From Concept to Context: Trends and Challenges, Proceedings of the 13th Annual KOTESOL International Conference*, 15–16 October, Seoul, Korea (pp. 91–98). https://koreatesol.org/sites/default/files/pdf_publications/KOTESOL-Proceeds2005web.pdf.

Liikkanen, L. A. (2012). Musical activities predispose to involuntary musical imagery. *Psychology of Music*, *40*(2), 236–256. https://doi.org/10.1177/0305735611406578.

Liikkanen, L. A., & Jakubowski, K. (2020). Involuntary musical imagery as a component of ordinary music cognition: A review of empirical evidence. *Psychonomic Bulletin and Review*, *27*, 1195–1217. https://doi.org/10.3758/s13423-020-01750-7.

Long, P., & Barber, S. (2015). Voicing passion: The emotional economy of songwriting. *European Journal of Cultural Studies*, *18*(2), 142–157. https://doi.org/10.1177/1367549414563298.

Lorenzutti, N. (2014). Beyond the gap fill: Dynamic activities for song in the EFL classroom. *English Teaching Forum*, *52*(1), 14–21. www.researchgate.net/publication/374090874.

Ludke, K. M. (2010). Songs and singing in foreign language learning. Doctoral dissertation, University of Edinburgh. Edinburgh College of Art thesis and dissertation collection. http://hdl.handle.net/1842/5500.

Ludke, K. M. (2018). Singing and arts activities in support of foreign language learning: An exploratory study. *Innovation in Language Learning and Teaching*, *12*(4), 371–386. https://doi.org/10.1080/17501229.2016.1253700.

Ludke, K. M., Ferreira, F., & Overy, K. (2014). Singing can facilitate foreign language learning. *Memory and Cognition*, *42*, 41–52. https://doi.org/10.3758/s13421-013-0342-5.

Ludke, K. M., & Morgan, K. A. (2022). Pop music in informal foreign language learning: A search for learner perspectives. *ITL: International Journal of Applied Linguistics*, *173*(2), 251–285. https://doi.org/10.1075/itl.21009.lud.

Mackenzie, L. (2021). Linguistic imperialism, English, and development: Implications for Colombia. *Current Issues in Language Planning*, *23*(2), 137–156. https://doi.org/10.1080/14664208.2021.1939977.

Mahboob, A. (2011). English: The industry. *Journal of Postcolonial Cultures and Societies*, *2*(4), 46–61.

Mäkelä, M. (2007). Knowing through making: The role of the artefact in practice-led research. *Knowledge, Technology and Policy*, *20*, 157–163. https://doi.org/10.1007/s12130-007-9028-2.

Maloy, L. (2018). The children's music quotient: Quantifying the childness of music recordings made for children. *International Research in Children's Literature*, *11*(1), 33–46. https://doi.org/10.3366/ircl.2018.0252.

Mannarelli, P., & Serrano, R. (2022). 'Thank you for the music': Examining how songs can promote vocabulary learning in an EFL class. *Language Learning Journal*, 1–15. https://doi.org/10.1080/09571736.2022.2092198.

Market Growth Reports (2023). *Global English Language Training (ELT) Industry Research Report 2023, Competitive Landscape, Market Size, Regional Status and Prospect.* www.marketgrowthreports.com/enquiry/request-sample/22379596.

McCarthy, M. (2021). Fifty-five years and counting: A half-century of getting it half-right? *Language Teaching, 54*(3), 343–354. https://doi.org/10.1017/S0261444820000075.

Miranda, D. (2013). The role of music in adolescent development: Much more than the same old song. *International Journal of Adolescence and Youth, 18*(1), 5–22. https://doi.org/10.1080/02673843.2011.650182.

Mishan, F. (2022). The global ELT coursebook: A case of Cinderella's slipper? *Language Teaching, 55*(4), 490–505. https://doi.org/10.1017/s0261444820000646.

Mobbs, A., & Cuyul, M. (2018). Listen to the music: Using songs in listening and speaking classes. *English Teaching Forum, 56*(1), 22–29. https://files.eric.ed.gov/fulltext/EJ1181086.pdf.

Moore, A. F. (2016). *Song Means: Analysing and Interpreting Recorded Popular Song.* Routledge.

Murphey, T. (1990). *Song and Music in Language Learning.* Peter Lang.

Murphey, T. (1992). The discourse of pop songs. *TESOL Quarterly, 26*(4), 770–774. https://doi.org/10.2307/3586887.

Murphey, T. (2009). Some crucial elements of learning ecologies of linguistic contagion. In G. R. Gonçalves, S. R. G. Almeida, V. L. M. O. Paiva, & A. S. Rodrigues-Júnior (eds.), *New Challenges in Language and Literature* (pp. 129–147). Faculty of Letters of UFMG (Federal University of Minas Gerais).

Murphey, T. (2013). *Music and Song-Resource Books for Teachers.* Oxford University Press.

Nelson, R. (2006). Practice-as-research and the problem of knowledge. *Performance Research, 11*(4), 105–116. https://doi.org/10.1080/13528160701363556.

Nettl, B. (2000). An ethnomusicologist contemplates musical universals. In N. L. Wallin, B. Merker, & S. Brown (eds.), *The Origins of Music* (pp. 463–472). MIT Press.

Nguyen, T. T. M., Marlina, R., & Cao, T. H. P. (2020). How well do ELT textbooks prepare students to use English in global contexts? An evaluation of the Vietnamese English textbooks from an English as an international language (EIL) perspective. *Asian Englishes, 23*(2), 184–200. https://doi.org/10.1080/13488678.2020.1717794.

Nizamani, A., & Shah, W. A. (2022). Textbooks as 'neoliberal artifacts': A critical study of knowledge-making in ELT industry. *Critical Discourse Studies,* 1–18. https://doi.org/10.1080/17405904.2022.2160364.

Ożóg, C. (2018). An interview with Liz and John Soars: Meet the authors. *IH (International House) Journal of Education and Development, 44*. http://ihjournal.com/an-interview-with-liz-and-john-soars-.

Palin, C., Morgan, H., Charrington, M., Casey, H., Heijmer, J., & Dilger, S. (2023). *Open Up: A Six-Level Course for Primary Education*. Oxford University Press. www.oup.es/open-up/.

Patel, A. D. (2008). *Music, Language, and the Brain*. Oxford University Press.

Patel, A. D. (2012). Language, music, and the brain: A resource-sharing framework. In P. Rebuschat, M. Rohrmeier, J. A. Hawkins, & I. Cross (eds.), *Language and Music as Cognitive Systems* (pp. 204–223). Oxford University Press.

Patel, M., Solly, M., & Copeland, S. (2023). *The Future of English: Global Perspectives*, ed. B. O'Sullivan & Y. Jin. British Council. https://shorturl.at/5wOQb.

Peng, M., Shi, Y., & Zhang, P. (2023). ELT coursebooks for primary school learners: A comparative analysis of songs. *Language Teaching for Young Learners, 5*(1), 59–84. https://doi.org/10.1075/ltyl.00031.pen.

Pennycook, A. (2007). ELT and colonialism. In J. Cummins & C. Davison (eds.), *International Handbook of English Language Teaching: Part I*. Springer International Handbooks of Education, vol. 11 (pp. 13–24). Springer Science+Business Media.

Pennycook, A. (2017). *The Cultural Politics of English as an International Language*. Taylor & Francis.

Ping, Q. (2018). Ideologies in primary English textbooks in China. In X. L. Curdt-Christiansen & C. Weninger (eds.), *Language, Ideology and Education: The Politics of Textbooks in Language Education* (pp. 163–180). Routledge.

Publishers Association (2019). *Publishers Association Yearbook 2019*. Publishers Association.

Ramadhania, V. A. (2022). Analyzing the use of double negatives in the lyrics of 15 English songs. *Etnolingual, 6*(2), 80–89. https://doi/10.20473/etno.v6i2.37071.

R'boul, H. (2022). ELT in Morocco: Postcolonial struggles, linguistic imperialism and neoliberal tendencies. In A. J. Daghigh, J. M. Jan, & S. Kaur (eds.), *Neoliberalization of English Language Policy in the Global South* (pp. 73–88). Springer International.

Roberts, D. F., Henriksen, L., & Foehr, U. G. (2009). Adolescence, adolescents, and media. In R. M. Lerner & L. Steinberg (eds.), *Handbook of Adolescent Psychology* (vol. 2, pp. 314–344). John Wiley. https://doi.org/10.1002/9780470479193.adlpsy002010.

Romero, P. (2017). Teaching and learning English through songs: A literature review. *MSU (Michigan State University) Working Paper in SLS (Second Language Studies) vol. 8*, 40–45. https://doi.org/10.17613/3j67-xe36.

Saldiraner, G., & Cinkara, E. (2021). Using songs in teaching pronunciation to young EFL learners. *PASAA: Journal of Language Teaching and Learning in Thailand, 62*, 119–141. https://doi.org/10.58837/chula.pasaa.62.1.5.

Saricoban, A., & Metin, E. (2000). Songs, verse and games for teaching grammar. *Internet TESL (Teaching English as a Second Language) Journal, 6*(10), 1–7. http://iteslj.org/Techniques/Saricoban-Songs.html.

Shen, C. (2009). Using English songs: An enjoyable and effective approach to ELT. *English Language Teaching, 2*(1), 88–94. https://doi.org/10.5539/elt.v2n1p88.

Shi, H., & Lim, F. V. (2022). English and Englishness: A multimodal analysis of English language teaching materials in contemporary China. In T. Xiong, D. Feng, & G. Hu (eds.), *Cultural Knowledge and Values in English Language Teaching Materials* (pp. 63–80). Springer. https://doi.org/10.1007/978-981-19-1935-0_4.

Smith, J. (2010). The books that sing: The marketing of children's phonograph records, 1890–1930. In D. Buckingham & V. Tingstad (eds.), *Childhood and Consumer Culture: Studies in Childhood and Youth* (pp. 90–108). Palgrave Macmillan.

Smith, S. G. (2009). Hooks. *Journal of Aesthetics and Art Criticism, 67*(3), 311–319. https://doi.org/10.1111/j.1540-6245.2009.01361.x.

Summer, T. (2018). An analysis of pop songs for teaching English as a foreign language: Bridging the gap between corpus analysis and teaching practice. In V. Werner (ed.), *The Language of Pop Culture* (pp. 187–209). Routledge.

Tegge, F. (2017). The lexical coverage of popular songs in English language teaching. *System, 67*, 87–98. http://dx.doi.org/10.1016/j.system.2017.04.016.

Tegge, F. (2018). Pop songs in the classroom: Time-filler or teaching tool? *ELT (English Language Teaching) Journal, 72*(3), 274–284. https://doi.org/10.1093/elt/ccx071.

Thompson, P., & Harding, P. (2019). Collective creativity: A 'service' model of commercial pop music production at PWL in the 1980s. In R. Hepworth-Sawyer, J. Hodgson, J. Paterson, & R. Toulson (eds.), *Innovation in Music: Performance, Production, Technology, and Business* (pp. 143–159). Routledge.

Tlili, Z. (2016). A critical chronotopic approach to lyrics of top-ranking popular songs in the UK. *Critical Discourse Studies, 13*(2), 228–246. https://doi.org/10.1080/17405904.2015.1103766.

Tomczak, E., & Lew, R. (2019). The song of words: Teaching multi-word units with songs. *3L: Southeast Asian Journal of English Language Studies, 25*(4), 16–33. https://doi.org/10.17576/3l-2019-2504-02.

Trinick, R. M. (2012). Sound and sight: The use of song to promote language learning. *General Music Today*, *25*(2), 5–10. https://doi.org/10.1177/1048371311402066.

Trotta, J. (2018). Pop culture and linguistics – Is that, like, a thing now? In V. Werner (ed.), *The Language of Pop Culture* (pp. 27–45). Routledge.

Turpin, M., & Stebbins, T. (2010). The language of song: Some recent approaches in description and analysis. *Australian Journal of Linguistics*, *30*(1), 1–17. https://doi.org/10.1080/07268600903133998.

Tyarakanita, A., Drajati, N. A., Rochsantiningsih, D., & Nurkamto, J. (2021). The representation of gender stereotypes in Indonesian English language textbooks. *Sexuality and Culture*, *25*(3), 1140–1157. https://doi.org/10.1007/s12119-021-09813-0.

UK Music (2021). *This Is Music*. www.ukmusic.org/wp-content/uploads/2022/05/This-Is-Music-2021-The-Impact-of-the-Music-Industry.pdf.

Upendran, S. (2001). Teaching phrasal verbs using songs. *Internet TESL (Teaching English as a Second Language) Journal*, *7*(7). http://iteslj.org/Techniques/Upendran-PhrasalVerbs.html.

Van Dijck, J. (2006). Record and hold: Popular music between personal and collective memory. *Critical Studies in Media Communication*, *23*(5), 357–374. https://doi.org/10.1080/07393180601046121.

Vestad, I. L. (2017). Introduction: Children's music – an emerging field of research. *Nordic Journal of Art and Research*, *6*(2). https://doi.org/10.7577/information.v6i2.2274.

Vestad, I. L., & Dyndahl, P. (2020). Musical gentrification, parenting and children's media music. In P. Dindahl, S. Karlsen, & R. Wright (eds.), *Musical Gentrification: Popular Music, Distinction, and Social Mobility* (pp. 66–79). Routledge.

Vinge, J. (2017). What is good and bad children's music? Exploring quality and value in music for children. *Nordic Journal of Art and Research*, *6*(2). https://doi.org/10.7577/information.v6i2.2278.

Watson, A., & Ward, J. (2013). Creating the right 'vibe': Emotional labour and musical performance in the recording studio. *Environment and Planning A*, *45*(12), 2904–2918. https://doi.org/10.1068/a45619.

Werner, V. (2012). Love is all around: A corpus-based study of pop music lyrics. *Corpora*, *7*(1), 19–50. http://dx.doi.org/10.3366/cor.2012.0016.

Westphal, M. (2021). Pop music and teaching English as an international language. In M. Callies, S. Hehner, P. Meer, & M. Westphal (eds.), *Glocalising Teaching English as an International Language: New Perspectives for Teaching and Teacher Education in Germany* (vol. 3, pp. 181–197). Routledge.

Whiting, C. (2023). Valuing in songwriting. *International Association for the Study of Popular Music (IASPM) Journal*, *13*(1), 140–156. https://doi.org/10.5429/2079-3871(2023)v13i1.8en.

Wolf, F., & Gibson, E. (2005). Representing discourse coherence: A corpus-based study. *Computational Linguistics*, *31*(2), 249–287. https://doi.org/10.1162/0891201054223977.

Wright, R. (2011). Musical futures: A new approach to music education. *Canadian Music Educator*, *53*(2), 19–21.

Yarmakeev, I. E., Pimenova, T. S., Abdrafikova, A. R., & Syunina, A. S. (2016). Folk songs do magic in teaching speech and grammar patterns in EFL class. *Journal of Language and Literature*, *7*(1), 235–240. https://doi.org/10.7813/jll.2016/7-1/43.

Yung, K. W. H. (2023). Engaging exam-oriented students in communicative language teaching by 'packaging' learning English through songs as exam practice. *RELC (Regional Language Centre) Journal*, *54*(1), 280–290. https://doi.org/10.1177/0033688220978542.

Zagorski-Thomas, S. (2014). Musical meaning and the musicology of record production. In D. Helms & T. Phleps (eds.), *Black Box Pop: Analysen populärer Musik* (pp. 135–148). Transcript Verlag. https://doi.org/10.14361/transcript.9783839418789.135.

Zbikowski, L. M. (2012). Music, language, and what falls in between. *Ethnomusicology*, *56*(1), 125–131. https://doi.org/10.5406/ethnomusicology.56.1.0125. See https://zbikowski.uchicago.edu/pdfs/Zbikowski_Response_to_Lawson_2012.pdf.

Acknowledgements

We are very grateful to Professor Rich Perks for his critical reading and helpful feedback.

Permissions

'Where's the Pencil Case?' from *Open Up 1* by Hawrys Morgan; 'Carnival Time' and 'What's in the Classroom?' from *Open Up 2* by Cheryl Palin; 'What Do You Do at the Weekend?' from *Open Up 3* by Helen Casey; 'There Was a Carnival' from *Open Up 5* by Sarah Dilger and Joanna Heijmer; and 'Bowling Alley' from *Open Up 6* by Sarah Dilger and Joanna Heijmer – all reproduced by permission of Oxford University Press © Oxford University Press (2023).

Cambridge Elements

Twenty-First Century Music Practice

Simon Zagorski-Thomas
London College of Music, University of West London

Simon Zagorski-Thomas is a Professor at the London College of Music (University of West London, UK) and founded and runs the 21st Century Music Practice Research Network. He is series editor for the Cambridge Elements series and Bloomsbury book series on 21st Century Music Practice. He is ex-chairman and co-founder of the Association for the Study of the Art of Record Production. He is a composer, sound engineer and producer and is, currently, writing a monograph on practical musicology. His books include *Musicology of Record Production* (2014; winner of the 2015 IASPM Book Prize), *The Art of Record Production: an Introductory Reader for a New Academic Field* co-edited with Simon Frith (2012), the *Bloomsbury Handbook of Music Production* co-edited with Andrew Bourbon (2020) and the *Art of Record Production: Creative Practice in the Studio* co-edited with Katia Isakoff, Serge Lacasse and Sophie Stévance (2020).

About the Series

Elements in Twenty-First Century Music Practice has developed out of the 21st Century Music Practice Research Network, which currently has around 250 members in 30 countries and is dedicated to the study of what Christopher Small termed musicking – the process of making and sharing music rather than the output itself. Obviously this exists at the intersection of ethnomusicology, performance studies, and practice pedagogy / practice-led-research in composition, performance, recording, production, musical theatre, music for screen and other forms of multi-media musicking. The generic nature of the term '21st Century Music Practice' reflects the aim of the series to bring together all forms of music into a larger discussion of current practice and to provide a platform for research about any musical tradition or style. It embraces everything from hip-hop to historically informed performance and K-pop to Inuk throat singing.

Cambridge Elements

Twenty-First Century Music Practice

Elements in the Series

The Marks of a Maestro: Annotating Mozart's 'Jupiter' Symphony
Raymond Holden and Stephen Mould

Chinese Street Music: Complicating Musical Community
Samuel Horlor

Reimagine to Revitalise: New Approaches to Performance Practices Across Cultures
Charulatha Mani

A Philosophy of Playing Drum Kit: Magical Nexus
Gareth Dylan Smith

Shared Listenings: Methods for Transcultural Musicianship and Research
Stefan Östersjö, Nguyễn Thanh Thủy,
David G. Hebert and Henrik Frisk

Repetition and Performance in the Recording Studio
Rod Davies

Original Pirate Material: The Streets and Hip-hop Transatlantic Exchange
Justin A. Williams

Cross-Cultural Collaboration in Popular Music: Practice-Based Research
Toby Martin, Seyed Mohammad Reza Beladi and Đặng Lan

What Musicking Affords: Musical Performance and the Post-cognitivist Turn
Marc Duby

Hidden Music: The Composer's Guide to Sonification
Milton Mermikides

More Than Words: Songs for the Language Classroom
Tom Parkinson and Luke Vyner

A full series listing is available at: www.cambridge.org/EMUP

For EU product safety concerns, contact us at Calle de José Abascal, 56–1°, 28003 Madrid, Spain or eugpsr@cambridge.org.

www.ingramcontent.com/pod-product-compliance
Lightning Source LLC
LaVergne TN
LVHW020350260326
834688LV00045B/1634